The
Private Prayers of
POPE
JOHN PAUL II

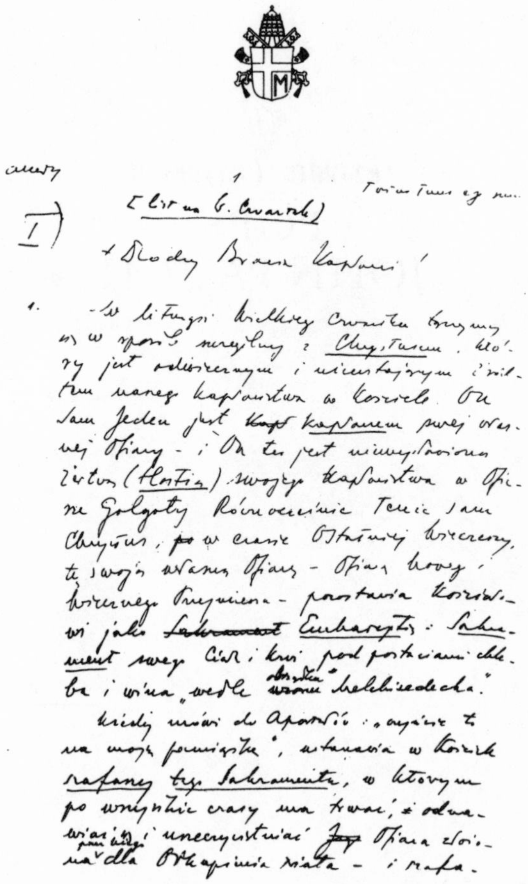
[List na W. Czwartek]

Totus Tuus ego sum

I)

+ Drodzy Bracia Kapłani!

1. W liturgii Wielkiego Czwartku łączymy się w sposób szczególny z Chrystusem, który jest odwiecznym i nieustającym źródłem naszego kapłaństwa w Kościele. On sam Jeden jest ~~Kapł~~ Kapłanem swej własnej Ofiary – i On też jest niewysłowioną Żertwą (Hostią) swojego Kapłaństwa w Ofierze Golgoty. Równocześnie Tenże Sam Chrystus, ~~po~~ w czasie Ostatniej Wieczerzy, tę swoją własną Ofiarę – Ofiarę Nowego i Wiecznego Przymierza – pozostawia Kościołowi jako ~~Sakrament~~ Eucharystię: Sakrament swego Ciała i Krwi pod postaciami chleba i wina, „wedle obrządku Melchizedecha".

Kiedy mówi do Apostołów: „czyńcie to na moją pamiątkę", ustanawia w Kościele szafarzy tego Sakramentu, w którym po wszystkie czasy ma trwać, odnawiać się i uobecniać ta Ofiara złożona dla Odkupienia świata – i szafa-

Reproduction of the first page of the manuscript of John Paul II's Letter to Priests, Holy Thursday, 1985.

The
Private Prayers of

POPE
JOHN PAUL II

Words of Inspiration

POCKET BOOKS
New York   London   Toronto   Sydney   Singapore

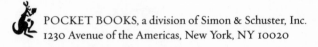
POCKET BOOKS, a division of Simon & Schuster, Inc.
1230 Avenue of the Americas, New York, NY 10020

Copyright © 1994 by Libreria Editrice Rogate
English language translation copyright © 2001 by Libreria Editrice Rogate
Translation by Ann Goldstein

Original Italian language edition published in Italy in 1994 by Libreria
Editrice Rogate, LLC as *Alpinisti dello Spirito*

Published under agreement with Compulsion Sub, LLC,
the exclusive world-wide licensee of the original Italian publication
of *The Private Prayers of Pope John Paul II*.

ISBN: 0-7434-4437-X

First Pocket Books hardcover printing November 2001

10 9 8 7 6 5 4 3 2 1

POCKET and colophon are registered trademarks of
Simon & Schuster, Inc.

For information regarding special discounts for bulk purchases,
please contact Simon & Schuster Special Sales at 1-800-456-6798
or business@simonandschuster.com

Book design by Lindgren/Fuller Design

Printed in the U. S. A.

This edition represents an English rendition of the original book *Alpinisti dello Spirito* ("Spiritual Mountaineers") published in Italian in the Vatican City State. It includes many of the Pope's words addressed to members of Secular Institutes, consecrated lay people who play a large part in the life of the Church. The work retains the organization of the Vatican edition.

Future works in this series will feature translations of additional volumes in the Vatican City series.

CONTENTS

INTRODUCTION

"Spiritual Mountaineers" is the evocative image created by Paul VI to indicate the difficult path of the consecrated in the Secular Institutes. So said Pope Paul, playing with words, as he addressed the "advance wing of the Church":

> *"You are in the world*
> *and not of the world,*
> *but for the world."*

And John Paul II, in his eagerness for new evangelization, is never tired of encouraging and promoting vocations for the Secular Institutes, observing that they have a mission of salvation to perform for mankind in our time. Society today has a need for men and women who, living in the world, though the world is unaware of the exterior signs, will open to it the pathways of Christian salvation, and who will mold it, perfect it, and sanctify it. Paul VI also said:

*"Modern man listens more willingly
to witnesses than to teachers,
or if he listens to teachers he does so
because they are witnesses."*

Well then, may the consecrated within the Secular Institutes pledge, by their witness, to remind the world that we
are in need not of better days but of men who will make our
days better!

My Heart
Opens to You

Dear members of the Secular Institutes,
it is an immense joy for me to meet you.
... I greet all the consecrated men and women
of the Secular Institutes.
This is an occasion to confirm you in your faith
and encourage you in your vocation
of unconditional dedication to the Lord,
with *"the joy of belonging exclusively to God,"*
since your entire existence
is a solemn response
to *"Follow me"* as a declaration of love.
This dedication must make you more sensitive
to the needs and sufferings of all men and women,
and, at the same time, more faithful to the Church.

CHILE, APRIL 3, 1987

My heart opens to you, dear members of lay institutes. You are exceptional witnesses of the absoluteness of God and the transcendence of the goods of the Kingdom of God over all other values. I fervently beg you to preserve the taste and smell of a genuine evangelical radicalism. Your life, which in itself expresses extraordinary praise of the grace of Christ and is an active sign of the dynamic presence of the Spirit, will then become a precious gift offered not only to the Christian community but also to that world which is ignorant of the magnitude of your vocation and your distinguished service.

PADUA, SEPTEMBER 12, 1982

I would like to express
my deepest esteem
for all the members of the Secular Institutes,
joined with a cordial greeting.
You have a special
type of consecration
and your own place in the Church.
Nourished on a solid spirituality,
you must be faithful to the call of Christ
and the Church,
so that you may be effective instruments of
    transformation
of the world from within.

MADRID, NOVEMBER 2, 1982

5

Dear brothers and sisters!

It is a joy for me—a joy that is renewed every time, with its freshness intact—to meet, in the course of my pastoral visits, those who have dedicated to Christ their full spiritual and physical energies, welcoming without reserve his call to commitment to the coming of the Kingdom of God.

Taking the words of the Apostle Paul as my own, I wish to repeat to you, today, with deep rapture: "*My love is with all of you in Jesus Christ.*"

It is you, members of the Secular Institutes, who in new ways, dictated by the requirements of the times, follow the same ideal, of being the evangelical yeast, added to the measure of flour "till it was all leavened."

BOLOGNA, APRIL 18, 1982

You are a great treasure of spirituality and apostolic initiative within the Church. *On you, in large part, the fate of the Church depends.*

This places on you a grave responsibility and requires you to be profoundly aware of the magnitude of the vocation you have received and of the need to be constantly more worthy of it. It means following Christ and, by responding affirmatively to the call, joyously serving the Church, in the holiness of life.

MADRID, NOVEMBER 2, 1982

What Are the
Secular Institutes?

Some special words of greeting and appreciation to you, the consecrated of the Secular Institutes, who have taken on the commitments of the consecrated life, as recognized by the Church, in a special form distinct from that which characterizes religious.

The Secular Institutes constitute a meaningful reality. The Church needs them in order to create an apostolate of profound Christian witness in the most varied areas, *"which can help to change the world from within, by becoming the life-giving leaven."*

I pray to the Lord that many may listen to his voice and follow him on this path. I beg you to remain faithful to your personal vocation, as it is *"characterized and unified by consecration, the apostolate, and secular life."*

MADRID, NOVEMBER 2, 1982

The Secular Institutes are intended to be a faithful expression of the ecclesiology that the Council* affirms when it points out the universal vocation to holiness; the innate duties of the baptized; the presence of the Church in the world, where it must act as the leaven and be *"the universal sacrament of salvation"*; the variety and dignity of different vocations; and the *"unique reverence"* that the Church has for *"perfect continence for the Kingdom of Heaven"* and for the testimony of evangelical poverty and obedience.

We must express profound thanks to the Father of infinite mercy, who has taken to heart the needs of humanity and who, with the living force of the Spirit, has launched in this century new initiatives for its redemption. To the Triune God may there be honor and glory for this eruption of grace, the Secular Institutes, through which he manifests his inexhaustible benevolence, and through which the Church itself loves the world in the name of the Lord God.

MAY 6, 1983

---

* Second Vatican Council.

The newness of the gift that the Spirit, in response to the exigencies of our time, has made to the eternal fruitfulness of the Church can be grasped only if the inseparability of the constituent elements is clearly understood: consecration and secularity; the resulting apostolate of testimony, Christian commitment to society, and evangelization; fraternity that, without being defined by a shared life, is a true communion; and the external form of life, which is not distinct from its environment.

Now, this vocation, so timely and I would say so urgent, has to be known and made known, as the vocation of people who consecrate themselves to God by practicing the evangelical counsels. They are people who strive to immerse their entire life and all their activities in that special consecration, making themselves totally available to the will of the Father and working to change the world from within.

In this way they will arouse generous responses to the difficult but beautiful vocation of "full consecration to God and his creatures." It is a demanding vocation, because it means bringing the commitments implicit in baptism to their most complete fulfillment in evangelical radicalism, and also because this evangelical life must be incarnated in a wide variety of situations.

MAY 6, 1983

The diversity of gifts entrusted to the Secular Institutes expresses the diversity of apostolic aims, which include all areas of human and Christian life. This pluralistic richness is also manifested in the many kinds of spirituality, and the diversity of sacred bonds, that animate the Secular Institutes, and that characterize different styles in the practice of the evangelical counsels and the many possible ways they can be integrated into the social environment. My predecessor, Pope Paul VI, who showed so much affection for the Secular Institutes, rightly said that if they *remain faithful to their vocation, they will be like an experimental laboratory, in which the Church tests the ways she relates concretely to the world.* Therefore, lend your support to these institutes, so that they can be faithful to the uniqueness of their founding charisms as recognized by the hierarchy, and be vigilant to discover in their fruits the lesson that God wants to give us for life and for the activity of the entire Church.

MAY 6, 1983

If Secular Institutes are developed and supported, the local Churches will benefit, too.

Also, with regard to its characteristics, a Secular Institute must identify and take on the pastoral urgencies of its particular Church, and authorize its members to be diligent participants in the hopes and duties, the plans and anxieties, the spiritual wealth and the limits, in a word: the communion of their specific Church. This must be a serious consideration for the Secular Institute, just as pastors must take care to recognize the nature of the institute and ask for its contribution accordingly.

Another responsibility falls upon the pastors: to offer to the Secular Institutes whatever doctrinal matter they need. These institutes are meant to be part of the world and to ennoble temporal reality, ordering and exalting it, so that everything aspires toward Christ as the head. Therefore the full wealth of Catholic doctrine on creation, the incarnation, and redemption must be given to the institutes, so that they may make God's wise and mysterious plans for humanity, for history, and for the world their own.

MAY 6, 1983

Changing the world "from within"

I would like to ask you to reflect on a resolution that is yours personally: *to change the world from within*. You are, in fact, integrated into the world completely, and not only in terms of your place in society; it is, above all, an essential inner attitude. You must therefore consider yourselves "part" of the world, pledged to sanctify it, fully accepting the requirements that derive from the legitimate autonomy of the world's realities, its values, and its laws.

This means that you must take seriously the natural order and its "ontological width," seeking to read in it the design freely followed by God, and offering your collaboration so that it may be realized progressively in history. Faith gives you indications of the higher destiny that Christ's initiative for salvation opens up for history; yet you will not find in the divine revelation perfect, ready answers to the numerous questions posed by your actual commitment. It is your duty to search, by the light of faith, for appropriate solutions to the practical problems that emerge from time to time, and you will not often find such solutions except by taking risks.

Thus you have a commitment to promote the realities of the natural order, and a commitment to interpolate the values of faith, and these commitments must be united with and harmoniously integrated into your life, constituting its basic orientation and its constant inspiration. In this way, you can contribute to changing the world "from within," becoming its life-giving leaven and obeying the charge that was given to you in the Motu Proprio *Primo feliciter*: to be "*the leaven, modest but efficient, which acting everywhere and always, and mixed into every class of citizens, from the humblest to the highest, strives to fill each and every one of them by example and in every way, until it permeates the entire mass and the whole takes shape and is transformed into Christ.*"

To the Secular Institutes,
August 28, 1980

The value of consecration in the world

Beloved brothers and sisters of the Secular Institutes!

You are qualified representatives of an ecclesial reality that has been, especially in this century, the sign of a special "motion" of the Holy Spirit within the Church of God. The Secular Institutes, in fact, have highlighted the value of consecration even for those who are working "in the world"; that is, for those who are engaged in worldly activities, both as secular priests and, above all, as lay people. For the laity, in fact, the history of the Secular Institutes marks an important stage in the development of the doctrine regarding the special nature of the lay apostolate, and in the recognition of the universal vocation of the faithful to holiness and the service of Christ.

Your mission today has a perspective consolidated by a theological tradition: this consists in the "*consecratio mundi,*" the consecrated life in the world—that is, by working from within, to lead back to Christ, as the sole head, all earthly realities.

I am pleased with the theme chosen for the present Assembly: "*The mission of the Secular Institutes in the world of 2000.*" This is a complex subject, which corresponds to the hopes and expectations of the Church in the near future.

The program is very stimulating for you, because it opens the horizons of the third millennium of Christ to your personal vocation and spiritual experience, with the purpose of helping you fulfill with ever-greater awareness your call to holiness while living in the world, and also helping you collaborate, by living your consecration inwardly and authentically, in the work of salvation and evangelization of all the people of God.

The impact of the third millennium of the Christian era is undoubtedly inspiring for those who intend to devote their lives to good and to the progress of humanity. We would all like the new era to correspond to the image that the Creator conceived for mankind. It is he who constructs history and leads it onward, as the story of mankind's salvation in every epoch. Each of us, therefore, is called to pledge himself to fulfill in the new millennium a new chapter in the history of Redemption.

You wish to contribute to the holiness of the world from within, living in the world, by working from within the very heart of earthly realities, in accordance with the law of the Church.

Yet in the condition of *secularity* you are *consecrated.* Here is the originality of your task: you are in full title *lay people;* but you are consecrated, you are bound to Christ by a special vocation, to follow him more nearly, to imitate him as the "Servant of God," in the humility of the vows of chastity, poverty, and obedience.

You are aware that you share with all Christians the dignity of being children of God, living limbs of Christ, incorporated into the Church, granted, through baptism, the common ministry of the faithful. But you have also received the message, intrinsically linked to that dignity: of commitment to holiness, to the perfection of charity. You have responded to the call of the evangelical counsels, in which the self is given to God and Christ with an undivided heart, and yields completely to the will and guidance of the Spirit. You put that commitment into practice, not from outside, separating yourself from the world, but from within the complex realities of work, culture, professional life, and social service of every kind. This means that your professional activities and the areas where you share earthly concerns with other lay people will be the proving ground, the challenge—the cross but also the call, the mission, and the moment of grace and communion with Christ, in which your spirituality begins and develops.

All this requires, as you well know, continuous spiritual progress in relation to mankind, to realities, and to history. It requires the capacity to grasp, in the small as well as the great doings of the world, *a presence,* that of Christ the Savior, who walks always beside man, even when man ignores him and denies him. It requires, too, that you pay continual attention to the significance, for salvation, of daily events, so that they can be interpreted in the light of faith and Christian principles.

It requires, therefore, profound union with the Church, and fidelity to her ministry. You are asked for total, loving adherence to her thought and her message, knowing that that is achieved by means of the special tie that binds you to her.

It does not mean that the proper autonomy of lay people in the world is diminished in relation to consecration; rather, it is a matter of placing their consecration in its proper light, so that it does not become weak or work in isolation. The dynamic of your mission, just as you intend, far from being estranged from the life of the Church, is united with it in charity.

Another fundamental requirement consists in a generous and conscious acceptance of the mystery of the Cross.

Every ecclesial action is objectively rooted in the work of salvation, in the redemptive action of Christ, and attains its power from the sacrifice of the Lord, from his blood spilled on the Cross. The sacrifice of Christ, always present in the work of the Church, constitutes her power and her hope, the most mysterious and greatest gift of grace. The Church is well aware that her history is a story of sacrifice and self-denial.

As consecrated lay people, you experience the truth of that every day in the area of activity and mission that each of you has led. You know what dedication that work requires in the struggle against oneself, against the world and its lusts; but it is the only way to achieve true inner peace, the peace that only Christ can and knows how to give.

This evangelical path, often traversed in solitude and suffering, is precisely the path that gives you hope, because in the Cross you are sure of being in communion with our Lord and Redeemer.

Do not be discouraged by the context of the Cross. It will aid and support you in spreading the work of redemption and bringing the sanctifying presence of Christ to your brothers and sisters. That attitude will make manifest the provident action of the Holy Spirit, which "blows where it wishes." It alone can rouse the forces, initiatives, and potent signs through which the work of Christ is brought to fulfillment.

Extending the gift of redemption to all the works of man is the mission that the Spirit has given you; it is a sublime mission, it requires courage, but it is always a cause of happiness for you, if you live in the fellowship of charity with Christ and your brothers and sisters.

The Church of 2000 therefore expects strong collaboration from you on the arduous path of sanctifying the world.

IV WORLD CONGRESS OF SECULAR INSTITUTES,
AUGUST 26, 1988

If they remain faithful
to their special vocation
the Secular Institutes will become
"the experimental laboratory"
in which the Church tests
the ways it relates
concretely to the world.
It is why the institutes must hear
the call of the apostolic exhortation
Evangelii nuntiandi
as if it were addressed particularly to them:
"Their task...
is to put to use
every Christian and evangelical possibility
latent but already
present and active
in the affairs of the world.
Their own field
of evangelizing activity
is the vast and complex world
of politics, society, and economics,
but also the world of culture,
of science and the arts,
of international life,
of the mass media."

PAUL VI, AUGUST 25, 1976

Surely you realize how important it is that your experience of life, characterized, and unified, by consecration, the apostolate, and secular life, unfolds within a healthy pluralism and in genuine fellowship: with the pastors of the Church and through participation in the evangelizing mission of all the people of God?

This does not, however, compromise the essential character of your special kind of consecration to Christ. Paul VI noted a methodologically important distinction: *"It does not mean, obviously, that the Secular Institutes, as such, should be charged with these tasks. That is the duty of each of their members. It is the duty of the institutes themselves to develop the conscience of their members to a maturity and openness that will push them to prepare eagerly for their chosen profession, so that they may later confront with authority, and in a spirit of evangelical detachment, the burdens and joys of social responsibility that Divine Providence will steer them toward."*

AUGUST 28, 1980

I would like to give
the consecrated people
who belong to the Secular Institutes
and Associations of Apostolic Life
encouragement to pursue
their commitment to evangelization
with ever-renewed generosity
and enthusiasm,
by living their consecration in the world,
in order to imbue with the Gospel
human affairs and institutions.

URUGUAY, MARCH 31, 1987

Come, Follow Me

"*Come and follow me!*" How beautiful these words are for all of you—who have consecrated yourselves to God utterly, for the love and glory of his Kingdom, as a sign of the *Lord's Covenant* with mankind.

For this reason you are called to be the sign of *God's Absolution*. "*All those who are called by God,*" as the Second Vatican Council says, "*to practice the evangelical counsels, and who faithfully profess them, are consecrated to the Lord in a special way, following Christ.*" And walking in the footsteps of Christ leads you to share with ever-increasing awareness in the mystery of his Passion, death, and Resurrection. If you can be witnesses of the Easter Mystery, in a society worn out by the lure of consumer goods, eroticism, the abuse of power, God our Lord will be present in the world.

Through consecration, leaving your family and giving up the creation of a family, you have offered yourselves exclusively to the "God who is love," to demonstrate how relative everything that exists in the world is. The Kingdom of God, whose "elevation over all earthly things" is expressed in the religious life, is not of this world. People are in need of this testimony of yours.

Consecrated to the love of God you are not lost to people— on the contrary. Instead of being fathers and mothers of a small family, with physical descendants, you are fathers and mothers with spiritual descendants, in a much larger family, the holy family of God, the Church, "Mother and Teacher" of peoples.

ANGOLA, JUNE 9, 1992

The various vocations in the lay state

The rich variety of the Church is manifested further within each state of life. Thus *within the lay state diverse "vocations" are presented,* or, rather, diverse paths in spiritual life and the apostolate are taken by individual members of the lay faithful. In the area of a "common" lay vocation "special" lay vocations flourish. In this context we should also note the spiritual experience that has developed recently in the Church with the flowering of various forms of Secular Institutes. These offer for the lay faithful, and for priests as well, the possibility of professing the evangelical counsels of poverty, chastity, and obedience through vows or promises, while completely maintaining their own state, lay or clerical. As the synodal Fathers have noted, *"The Holy Spirit generates other forms of self-giving, to which people who remain fully in the lay state can devote themselves."*

We can conclude by rereading a beautiful passage from St. Francis of Sales, who promoted lay spirituality so well. Speaking of "devotion," or, rather, of Christian perfection, or "life according to the Spirit," he explains in a simple yet insightful way the vocation of all Christians to holiness and, at the same time, the specific form in which individual Christians fulfill it: *"In the creation God commanded the plants to bring forth their fruits, each one 'after its kind.' So does he command all*

Christians, who are the living plants of his Church, to bring forth the fruits of devotion, each according to his state and his character. Devotion must be practiced in a different way by the gentleman, by the workman, by the servant, by the prince, by the widow, by the unmarried woman and the married one. That is not sufficient, but the practice of devotion must also be adapted to the strength, the employment, and the duties of each one in particular.... It is an error, or rather a heresy, to try to banish the devout life from the regiment of soldiers, the mechanics' workshop, the court of princes, or the homes of married people. It is true, Philotea, that a purely contemplative, monastic, and religious devotion cannot be exercised in those states, but, besides these three types of devotion, there are several others adapted to bring perfection to those who live in the secular state. Therefore, wherever we are, we can and should aspire to the perfect life."

Along the same lines, the Second Vatican Council states: "*This lay spirituality should take its particular character from the circumstances of one's state in life (married and family life, celibacy, or widowhood), from one's state of health, and from one's professional and social activity. All must not cease to cultivate the qualities and talents bestowed on them in accord with those conditions, and should make use of the gifts they have received from the Holy Spirit.*"

What is valid for spiritual vocations is also valid, and in a certain sense with greater reason, for the infinite ways in which all the members of the Church are laborers in the vineyard of the Lord, building up the mystical body of Christ. Truly each one, with his unique and singular personal history, is called by name, to bring his own contribution to the coming of the

Kingdom of God. No talent, no matter how small, is to be hidden or left unutilized.

In this regard, the Apostle Peter gives us a stern warning: *"As each has received a gift, employ it for one another, as good stewards of God's varied grace."*

CHRISTIFIDELES LAICI, 56

The lay faithful and their secular character

The lay faithful *"live in the world, that is, in every one of the secular professions and occupations, and in the ordinary situations of family and social life, from which the very fabric of their existence is woven."* They are persons who live an ordinary life in the world, they study, they work, they form relationships as friends, professionals, members of society, cultures, etc. The Council considers their state to be not simply an exterior and environmental framework but, rather, a reality destined to find in Jesus Christ the fullness of its meaning. Indeed, it leads to the affirmation that *"the Word made flesh willed to share in human fellowship.... He sanctified those human ties, especially family ones, in which social relations arise, willingly submitting to the laws of his country. He chose to lead the life of an ordinary craftsman of his own time and place."*

The "world" thus becomes the place and the means for the lay faithful to fulfill their Christian vocation, because the world itself is destined to glorify God the Father in Christ.

CHRISTIFIDELES LAICI, 15

In a special way, your vocation is *knowing how to taste* the divine realities and being *expert* in them. This tends to give a supernatural "taste" to your life, to your speech. And so it will allow you to give a supernatural taste to the realities of this world. It means that you must be exemplary *cultivators of knowledge,* understood not only and not so much as human knowledge but also and above all as a *gift of the Holy Spirit.*

Never forget this responsibility of yours. If a food is tasteless, salt can give it flavor. But if the salt itself has lost its taste, as Jesus points out to us, "how will you season it?" If knowledge of the Holy Spirit is lacking, nothing can replace it. And you are called on in a special way to taste this knowledge and make it tasty to men.

You are called on to enrich the world in spite of your poverty. And how is that possible? By imitating the prophet Elijah.

We may recall two things about him, which he clearly possessed, and which made him great: consciousness of his *human limits* and knowledge of a *divine power* in which he put complete trust and of which, as a prophet, he intended to be the instrument and spokesman.

Similarly, dear brothers and sisters, you have been specially called among the people of God to this dual knowledge, this wisdom and this prophetic spirit, which speaks in the name of God and proclaims the word of God to all men and in particular, with preferential love, the poor and the humble. You, too, even in the desert that, as for Elijah, seems to take away all hope—I refer to widespread indifference and coldness, to the scarcity of vocations—you, too, must trust in the power of the word of God, on which your own word is based, your witness: so you will prepare for the triumph of good.

May the Blessed Virgin Mary, who beside the Cross of her Son profoundly lived this law of Christian hope, gain for us the *spirit of prophecy*, so that we may overcome the difficulties of the present and look serenely to the future.

PARMA, JUNE 7, 1988

In the midst of the people of God, you are and must be in a special way the *men and women of the temple*. Your vocation, in fact, binds you closely to the "house of the Lord" and to the "place where his glory dwells."

Your vocation of leading men to God is truly wonderful; as you are well aware, however, it involves a *responsibility*. The words of the Psalmist are famous:

> *Who shall ascend the hill of the LORD?*
> *And who shall stand in his holy place?*
> *He who has clean hands and a pure heart,*
> *who does not lift up his soul to what is false,*
> *and does not swear deceitfully.*
> *He will receive blessing from the LORD,*
> *and vindication from the God of his salvation.*

The purer and more blameless your life is, and the more consistent your behavior with the prayers you raise to the Almighty, the better able will you be to make our contemporaries, so many of whom have been led astray by the world's indifference, understand the importance and, indeed, the necessity of divine worship, both interior and exterior. You must restore to the men and women of today knowledge of, and taste and respect for, the holy place, where the Christian community, with the priest presiding, celebrates and worships the *mystery of the Eucharist*.

VERONA, APRIL 16, 1988

The faithful Virgin invites you today to consider *the marvels* that the Omnipotent has worked in you. A common grace, which flowers in each according to his own vocation and charism, brings you together and unites you. All of you have been called to Christ. The vocation flowered in your life as a gesture of God's partiality, as an invitation to total love for him.

Yes, the person of Christ lured you, his "Come and follow me" seduced you. The vocation to the consecrated life is a fundamental call to follow Christ, to live the mystery of his grace, to live in fellowship with him, to imitate him. It is a call to proclaim the Gospel with your own life, each according to Christ's individual call, and all together in the Church: so that the Bride of Christ in her nuptial garment—charity, the evangelical counsels, the beatitudes of the divine Teacher—may shine with the beauty of the Gospel made the word of life. And so the Church may be the living Christ who, present in the world today, continues the work of salvation through the consecrated, proclaiming the Good News through their words and gestures, their lives.

To live and communicate the grace of salvation with unconditional devotion is to contemplate every day the wonders of God's love in the present moment, in the mystery of your life and the Church.

VENEZUELA, JANUARY 28, 1985

I would like to underline yet again a fundamental point: which is that the ultimate fulfillment of reality is in charity. "*Who abides in love abides in God, and God abides in him.*" Also, the ultimate purpose of every Christian vocation is charity; in the institutes of consecrated life, the practice of the evangelical counsels becomes the main road leading to God, the supremely beloved, and to your brothers and sisters, who have all been called to the divine filiation.

Now, within a formative commitment, charity finds expression, support, and maturation in fraternal communion so that it can become testimony and action.

In your institutes, because of the demands of being inserted in the world, as postulated by your vocation, the Church does not require the communal life that is, on the other hand, proper to religious institutions. Yet it does require a "fraternal communion rooted and founded in charity," which makes its members "a single special family"; it requires that the members of a Secular Institute "*preserve their communion by paying careful attention to unity of spirit and true fraternity.*"

If people breathe this spiritual atmosphere, which assumes the broadest ecclesial communion, the developing commitment will not fail to achieve its purpose.

Every Christian formation is open to the fullness of life of the children of God, in such a way that the subject of our activity is, in essence, Jesus himself: "*It is no longer I who live, but Christ who lives in me.*" But this is true only if each of us can say: "*I have been crucified with Christ,*" Christ "*who gave himself for me.*"

It is the sublime law of the followers of Christ: embrace the Cross. The formative path cannot be cut off from that.

May the Virgin Mary be an example to you in this as well. She who—as the Second Vatican Council notes—*"while she lived on earth the life common to all, full of work and attention to the family... advanced in the pilgrimage of the faith and faithfully preserved her union with her Son unto the cross."*

AUGUST 28, 1984

Making the Lord of Life present

I am here to counsel you
to believe most fervently
in your vocation.
With all your being, love
your consecration.
I ask you to reaffirm God
in today's world,
to proclaim the Lord's preeminence
over every reality,
to bear witness with your life to
faith in the supreme and eternal values,
to lead man to discover
his dignity and responsibility,
to make manifest
the full actuality of the beatitudes.
All this in the simplicity,
in the humility,
in the indestructible joy
of a dedicated life.

BARI, FEBRUARY 26, 1984

With particular affection I urge the consecrated to engage voluntarily in an examination of their life. As people totally consecrated to God and the Church by their vocation, they must live in the rhythm of "giving-receiving." If they have received much, they must give much. The richness of their spiritual life and the generosity of their apostolic devotion create a favorable atmosphere for the revelation of other vocations. Their testimony and their cooperation are in accord with the loving arrangements of divine Providence.

MESSAGE FOR WORLD DAY OF PRAYER
FOR THE VOCATIONS, 1982

The path to holiness

Wherever you are in the world, you are with your vocation "to the universal Church" through your mission "in a particular local Church." Therefore, your vocation to the universal Church is fulfilled within the structure of the local Church. Every effort must be made to develop "the consecrated life" in the individual local Churches, so that it may contribute to their spiritual edification, and so that it may become their special power. Unity with the universal Church, through the local Church: this is your path.

NOVEMBER 24, 1978

The Consecrated Life

The consecrated life belongs inseparably to the structure and the sanctity of the Church.

It is *prophecy:* following, in fact, Christ chaste, obedient, and poor, those who are consecrated anticipate the coming of the Kingdom and underline the primacy of God over every other human interest, however legitimate. It is the *answer* to the inner demand to follow the divine Teacher on the narrow path of the beatitudes, in virginity and in giving oneself exclusively to God. It is the *exercise* of total fidelity to Christ and of diligent availability to man. Fidelity to God and fidelity to man: These are the poles of reference that guide you in searching out and following new pathways of evangelization and of human progress, with a broad missionary range.

It is only realistic to observe that, unfortunately, because you are always fewer and are able to count only rarely on promising vocational prospects, you are prevented from accomplishing all the good that you would like to. Fear not! *If you truly love Christ, he will not leave you without the forces you need,* and he will not allow his works to remain without strong followers. But you must *be faithful to the word that has been given!* Every day prolong the time you spend in intimate spiritual encounter with your mystical Bridegroom! Stay in his company: Then you will feel all the intensity of the gift that has been bestowed on you and will appreciate the high privilege he has given you of serving among the poor. Be persevering in praise, love, and joy, with a humble and grateful soul.

And with your heart expanded by the force of the spirit, you cannot help but make the voice of the man who is suffering your voice, you will be unable not to hear his cry of pain and distress. If you become incarnate in the human reality around you, you will easily understand how hard it is for people to live and follow the dictates of the Gospel.

Your house must be welcoming and your work marked by serene and disinterested dedication. If you work closely with the other members of the ecclesial community, examples of youthful commitment and of voluntary service will surely multiply around you: there are living and generous forces to be inspired and directed to the universal missionary task.

Display the joy of your consecration to all people; serve Christ among your brothers and sisters with a cheerful countenance. By bringing to fruition your special spirituality, be *the leaven of apostolic renewal* in society.

May Mary, Virgin and Mother of the Church, be your model and protect you always.

POTENZA, APRIL 28, 1991

Dear friends, while all who have been baptized participate in the mission of the Church, the Lord Jesus has called you to offer public witness of the Gospel in a way that distinguishes you. Your religious consecration is a special source of spiritual vitality for the Church. It leads to a way of life that serves the people of God through fidelity to a particular charism or to a particular spiritual inheritance. However, as I have had occasion to say elsewhere:

> "Even if the many apostolic works
> that you undertake
> are extremely important,
> nevertheless the truly *fundamental*
> work of the apostolate
> is *always what*
> (and at the same time *who*)
> you are in the Church."

BOTSWANA,
SEPTEMBER 13, 1988

The transparency of Christ

You must make Christ present by unreservedly welcoming the radical spirit of the beatitudes, aware that the consecrated life is "a privileged means for effective evangelization."

A sense of participation in the life of the Church will be fostered in those who are integrated into various activities and comforted by prayer. It is good to observe your growing conviction that you are members of God's people with a special vocation to consecration. It is good to see in you the Church as the virgin who awaits her bridegroom with the lighted lamp, a light for others and living witness of the values of the Kingdom.

This desire to be the transparency of Christ for others places you in a position of great importance and dignity, as men and women consecrated in the Church for the good of all humanity. Your duties have a profound ecclesiastical and social impact, since you can offer something of your own, that is, the gifts of a rich spirituality and a vast capacity for disinterested love. From the perspective of your integration into the Church, I encourage you to rejoice in your special presence, in full and faithful communion with the hierarchy, since there cannot be a genuine integration into the Church outside of the center of communion, which is the bishop in his diocese. Thus you will be the true light, the light of Christ in his Church, light that radiates its own self-fulfillment.

PARAGUAY, MAY 17, 1988

Consecrated to God, through Christ the Bridegroom, in the charity of the Holy Spirit, you must make your lives shine with the light and transparency of loving and serving Jesus.

Yes. Following Jesus is the essence and, so to speak, the crown of the religious life: "... *Go, sell what you possess and give to the poor, and you will have treasure in heaven; and come, follow me.*" Your prophetic presence as consecrated people in the world, in accordance with the charism of your institute, will be a permanent, hopeful sign of this evangelical following, being, in particular, light and salt, the sign and stimulus that distinguish the spirit of the Sermon on the Mount.

BOLIVIA, MAY 10, 1988

You must be the "image" of God

All those who are consecrated to the Lord join the group of living witnesses to the existence of this "Other," to a reality so "different" from the reality that can be verified by the senses; and their whole life, individually and in the community, is committed to the objective of recalling men who have been led astray from the reality of the supreme Good by the temptations of material goods, and reminding them of the allure of values that are not visible but are true and higher.

The new society of love cannot be built in the future unless the quality of love changes. You are the privileged sign of this new love that is destined to change the world. Your love, "different" from other loves, is the image of the love of God. And so your life, lived and dedicated according to the Gospel, becomes, through your sincere and pure love for men, convincing testimony of the love of the Father who is in Heaven.

ALBANO, SEPTEMBER 19, 1982

Through the initiative of the Savior and your generous response, *Christ* has become *the purpose of your existence and the center of all your thoughts.* For Christ you have professed the evangelical counsels; and Christ will sustain you in full faithfulness to Him and in loving service to his Church.

Religious consecration is essentially *an act of love:* the love of Christ for you and, in return, your love for him and for all his brothers and sisters. This mystery is proclaimed today in the Gospel when Jesus says to his disciples: *"As the Father has loved me, so have I loved you; abide in my love."* Christ wants you to abide in him, by being nourished by him daily in the celebration of the Eucharist and by giving your life back to him through prayer and self-denial. Trusting in his word and putting faith in his mercy, you respond to his love; you choose to follow him more nearly in chastity, poverty, and obedience, with the desire to participate more fully in the life and holiness of the Church. You wish to love as brothers and sisters all those whom Christ loves.

PHILIPPINES, FEBRUARY 17, 1981

In order for you members of the institutes of active life to make the religious side of your lives visible and productive, it is important that you reflect seriously on the goal of reaching a genuine synthesis between action and contemplation. I know that you work tirelessly for evangelization and that you serve your brothers and sisters according to the Gospel; I know that you work in all the areas where the Church is. Far from distancing you, this requires that your apostolic activity be permeated by God; that you pursue it with the purest intentions and in a spirit that radiates harmony and fraternity, excluding no one.

To be consecrated in the sphere of daily work you have to feel an urgent need to find and love God in your actions. Your work and true contemplation cannot be in opposition, which means that you have to work for God and with God, that you have to work with him and find him in your work. Certainly this requires, in turn, that you find special moments of intimacy with the Lord—these are indispensable. Contemplation leads to apostolic action, and action increases the value of those moments dedicated explicitly to prayer and contemplation.

Every consecrated soul is, ultimately, contemplative.

CHILE, APRIL 3, 1987

Professionals of holiness

The challenges of the new evangelization need the experienced contributions and generous support of all of you who are exclusively dedicated, by your religious profession, to God and the Church.

You are "witnesses of the Absolute," who have given up everything for the Kingdom of Heaven.

You well know that your first gift to the ecclesial community is the *testimony of consecration* that binds you to the Lord through the public and consistent profession of the vows of poverty, chastity, and obedience.

The Christian community and lay society consider you "professionals of holiness," and expect you to be concrete examples of faithfulness to Christ and love for your brothers and sisters.

Be men and women who everywhere spread feelings of communion and hope; make available to all, with humility and in a spirit of service, the unique talents that God has given you.

Joyfully proclaim the Resurrection of Christ. And if Jesus is truly risen in you and alive in your existence, you will bear witness that he is living. When his merciful and comforting action is felt, when he gives you the strength to open yourselves to others, to be available to your brothers and sisters with a free and undivided heart, to forgive them and bring them joy, then you understand fully that the Redeemer lives. You become capable of proclaiming him whatever the sacrifice. Even death.

LATINA, SEPTEMBER 29, 1991

You souls who are consecrated by professing the evangelical counsels, living in the world you constitute its spiritual leaven with the testimony of your life.

JUNE 26, 1986

You bring to life in yourself
the awareness and the joy
of your state as a consecrated person:
Christ must be the purpose
and the measure of your life.
Your vocation originates
in an encounter with him:
faith in him has determined
the "yes" of your commitment;
hope for his help
now supports
its enduring fulfillment;
the love that he has kindled in your hearts
nourishes the strength needed
for overcoming
the inevitable difficulties
and for the daily renewal
of your offering.

JANUARY 12, 1980

Participation in Christ's mission

Brothers and sisters, Christ is the purpose and the measure of our life. Your vocation had its origin in knowing Christ; and your life is sustained by his love. For he has called you to follow him more nearly with a consecrated life, through the gift of the Gospel's teachings. You follow him with sacrifice and spontaneous generosity. You follow him with joy, *"singing with gratitude to God from your heart psalms, hymns, and spiritual canticles."* And you follow him with faith, even considering it an honor to suffer humiliations in his name.

Your religious consecration is in essence an act of love. It is an imitation of Christ, who gave himself to his Father to save the world. In Christ love for the Father and love for men are united. And so it is for you. Your religious consecration has not only reinforced the baptismal gift of union with the Trinity but has also called you to greater service to the people of God. You are closer to the person of Christ, and participate more fully in his mission to save the world.

OCTOBER 4, 1979

The Secular Institutes
today constitute a
very precious presence
in the heart of the world
and a commitment to the Church.
They help lay people
strive for holiness
through temporal tasks,
in a profound union of
prayer and action.

MADAGASCAR,
APRIL 30, 1989

The Evangelical Counsels

Dear brothers and sisters, you have chosen the consecrated life by answering Christ's call to be perfect as *"our heavenly Father is perfect,"* and, to achieve that, you have undertaken the evangelical life of chastity, poverty, and obedience.

You must know that you have an irreplaceable role in the mission of the Church. With the renunciations that your vocation requires, *you bear witness to the primacy of spiritual values* and, in a certain sense, are a living invitation to your brothers and sisters to defend those values, values that they, today, may be more tempted to neglect. Through prayer and your life of union with God, you demonstrate the source of the effectiveness of all work for the coming of the Kingdom: *"If you dwell in me and my words dwell in you, ask what you will and it will be given to you."*

Continue to spread the joy that comes from choosing a *simple life,* in accordance with the beatitudes, and to *set an example of work:* we all have to work; work is how we earn a living, but it is also a source of pride, because it links man to the divine, ongoing work of creation.

GUINEA, FEBRUARY 24, 1992

In a world in which people struggle for power and wealth, in which the human body itself, disconnected from genuine love, has lost meaning, the commitment expressed in the evangelical counsels to follow Jesus Christ more nearly is more than ever prophetic. In the face of injustice and violence, in the face of the materialism that destroys human dignity, you who are faithful to the Church embrace a path based on dedication to Christ, poor, pure, and obedient. "*The rich man is not the one who possesses but the one who gives, who is capable of giving himself.*"

This shedding of every form of pride and human power determines relations between people, offering an alternative that, inspired by the beatitude, must be lived in your communities. "*The world needs the true 'contradiction' of religious consecration, as the permanent leaven of redemptive renewal.... It needs this testimony of love, it needs the testimony of the Redemption, as it is inscribed in the profession of the evangelical counsels.*"

Your life is a call to orient the future of mankind and the world, from this moment, to the same perspective as the values of the Kingdom. Your behavior in the world must remind people that the evangelical requirement to earn one's living by offering one's life for love continues to be valid. Christian witness, inseparably joined to the fulfillment of vows and to evangelical commitment, must push to broaden the horizon of human aspirations and reject any ideology that tries to subject it to the dictates of a materialistic vision of man and the world. Those who have been consecrated "*by their state bear witness, in a splendid and singular way, that the world cannot be transfig-*

ured and offered to God without the spirit of the beatitudes." And so, "*in the face of all these threatening forces, we have decided to be poor, poor like Christ, the Son of God and Savior of the world, poor like St. Francis, the eloquent image of Christ, poor like so many great souls who have illumi-nated the path of mankind.*"

CHILE, APRIL 3, 1987

You have left everything to follow Christ, in accordance with the evangelical counsels. You have chosen a state of life that allows you to embody them daily. This religious profession belongs inseparably to the life and sanctity of the Church.

In a world that knows so many kinds of slavery, and where one is easily encumbered with unnecessary wealth, you can demonstrate the radicalism and freedom of the Gospel, the obedience and poverty of Christ.

In a world that is bound to the immediate, that limits its horizon to earthly realities, that is intoxicated with its own conquests or, on the contrary, is in despair, you proclaim the Kingdom of God to come.

In a world that doubts, and seems far from God, you demonstrate that to love it freely is worthwhile; from now on, you dedicate to it in a special way all the resources of your heart. And you are free, through prayer in the heart of the Church, or through the many kinds of apostolic service to the Christian community that demand total availability.

I think at the same time of all those who, in the Secular Institutes, dedicate their lives to God.

BELGIUM, MAY 18, 1985

Many people in our time seem to live without concerning themselves with God, and in fact they deny the transcendent dimension of human existence. That denial gives force to the phenomenon of secularization, making man poorer in humanity. Thanks to the practice of the evangelical counsels of poverty, chastity, and obedience, you remind us, instead, of the teaching of Jesus: *"Take heed, and beware of all covetousness; for a man's life does not consist in the abundance of his possessions."* You recall to our contemporaries that our greatest misfortune is to bind our existence solely to material goods, for these perish, and our ultimate destiny does not depend on them.

Dear brothers and sisters,
may you be
in your lives
witnesses and prophets
of evangelical radicalism!

CASERTA,
MAY 24, 1992

More than ever, our world needs to discover, in your communities and your way of life, the value of a simple life in the service of the poor. It needs to know the value of a life freely pledged to *celibacy* to preserve itself for Christ and, with him, to love especially the unloved. It needs to know the value of a life in which obedience and fraternal community silently challenge the excesses of an independence that is sometimes capricious and sterile.

Above all, the world needs testimony of the *generosity of God's love.* Among those who doubt God or believe that he is absent, you are the demonstration that it is worthwhile to seek the Lord and love him for himself, that it is worthwhile to consecrate one's life to the Kingdom of God, and its apparent foolishness. Your lives thus become a sign of the indestructible faith of the Church. The free gift of one's life to Christ and to others is perhaps the most pressing challenge to a society in which money has become an idol. Your choice confounds, raises questions, lures, or annoys this world, but never leaves it indifferent. The Gospel is always, and in every way, a sign of contradiction.

> But *never be afraid to demonstrate*
> *your devotion to the Lord.*
> It does honor to you!
> It honors the Church!
> You have a specific place in the body of Christ,
> in which each of you must fulfill
> his own task,
> his own charism.

If, with the Holy Spirit, you seek the *holiness* that corresponds to your state of life, have no fear. He will not abandon you. Vocations will come to you.

And you yourselves will preserve your youthfulness of spirit, which has nothing to do with age. Yes, live in hope. Keep your eyes fixed on Christ and walk firmly in his footsteps, in joy and peace.

CANADA, SEPTEMBER 19, 1984

The celibate life
that you have chosen for the Kingdom of Heaven
makes you freer
for communion with Christ
and for service to men.
But *it makes you even freer*
for a close and profound
union among yourselves.
Do not let anything or anyone
tempt you to renounce
or diminish
this generous availability.
Indeed, make it more fruitful
through your life
and through service
on behalf of man's salvation.

AUSTRIA, SEPTEMBER 13, 1983

As consecrated people, you are consecrated above all and specifically by the profession and practice of the evangelical counsels; thus your life must offer an essentially evangelical witness. You must continually address yourselves to Christ, the living Gospel, and reproduce him in your life, in your way of thinking and working.

You are poor as Christ is poor; obedient, taking on that aspect of the heart of Christ, who came to redeem the world doing not his will but the will of the Father who sent him. Consequently you live the perfect measure for the Kingdom of Heaven, as a sign and stimulus of charity and as a source of apostolic fruitfulness in the world. The world today needs to see living examples of people who have left everything and embraced, as their ideal, life according to the evangelical counsels. It is true sincerity in you as the radical followers of Christ that will attract vocations to your institutes, because the young are looking for precisely this evangelical radicalism.

The Gospel is definitive and does not change. Its principles are forever. You cannot come up with "rereadings" of the Gospel according to the times, accommodating yourselves to what the world demands. On the contrary, the signs of the times and the problems of today's world should be read in the unfailing light of the Gospel.

MADRID, NOVEMBER 2, 1982

You work for the Kingdom of God

By your commitment to perfect charity, you express the hope of the Church and become its crown and glory. You are its comfort. You are its ambassadors.

As people already consecrated to God by baptism, you bear special witness to Christ in the Church and in the world with your renunciation—for the Kingdom of Heaven—of marriage, of the goods of this earth, and of the exercise of your free will. With your vows, you have made this sacrifice freely, for love of God and your neighbor, in a spirit of devotion and service.

Consecration to chastity has great value as a testimonial in a world pervaded by selfishness and the abuse of sex. Poverty calls on men not to be attached to money and the things that money can buy. Obedience must be practiced in contrast to rebellion, pride, vanity, and oppression. As the Second Vatican Council said, the religious state demonstrates that the Kingdom of Christ, whose requirements are paramount, is beyond all earthly concerns.

Even more important than your works is the life that you lead. You are consecrated persons who seek to follow Christ with intense love.

NIGERIA, FEBRUARY 15, 1982

Called to a special imitation of Christ

You, too, dear brothers and sisters, must preserve intact that "oblative will," with which you generously responded to the invitation of Jesus to follow him more nearly on the road toward Calvary, by means of the *sacred ties,* which bind you to him in *chastity, poverty, and obedience:* these vows constitute a synthesis through which Christ wishes to express himself, undertaking—through your response—a decisive struggle against the spirit of this world. *Chastity,* embraced for the Kingdom of Heaven, frees the heart in a special way, kindling in it ever-increasing charity toward God and one's brothers and sisters. *Poverty,* willingly embraced so that we may join Christ's following, makes us share in his poverty, for, though he was rich, he became poor for our sake, so that by his poverty we might become rich. *Obedience*—in which the will totally consecrated to God is offered as a sacrifice of oneself—unites us with the will that brings salvation.

FEBRUARY 2, 1981

In a world that too often seeks satisfaction in material well-being and the accumulation of power, a world that pursues happiness without any reference to God, *you are symbols who return to higher values.* Your identification with Christ and your observance of the evangelical dictates recall Christ's words: *"My kingdom is not of this world."* You are the ambassadors of he who proclaimed the message of the beatitudes, which inaugurated a "new" life that our contemporaries seek but do not always know how to find. They long for a new world, without want or war, without the threat of nuclear destruction, without the atrocities and injustices that debase human life; but they do not always recognize the profundity of *conversion* and reconciliation which such a metamorphosis requires. This is the wisdom that you must deepen through prayer and contemplation, so as to share it generously with *"any one who calls you to account for the hope that is in you."*

I greet each one of you. I take joy in your faith and I pray that generous men, women, and young people *"may see your good deeds"* and follow in your footsteps for the glory of our Father who is in Heaven.

FINLAND, JUNE 6, 1989

Open your consecrated hearts to love! Give yourselves, offer your-selves generously to mankind in our time! Open the doors of your houses to those who knock, asking for a more immediate and vivid experience of the light of the Gospel, so that through your testimony they may gain knowledge of the new life brought by the Resurrection!

You must become more and more aware that you are *qualified intermediaries* between merciful God and man the pilgrim of truth, justice, and peace. Strong as a result of the consecration of your life, you must know how to confront with courage the troubles of the world, the selfishness that denies love and violates justice, the error that disturbs and confounds souls.

You are called on to be the face of Christ, because the conscious, free offering of all you possess—in fact, of all that you are—repeats and articulates in the present the daily miracle of the love of the Son of God, who came to save every man and free him from evil.

Love cannot stop halfway, as you well know. Love must be ready to offer itself to the extreme limits of generosity. Jesus does not hesitate to demand perfection in this desire: "*You, therefore, must be perfect, as your heavenly Father is perfect.*"

Never forget that you are "the gift of God to others." Love others as Christ loved you. Love according to the rule that Christ himself established: "*So whatever you wish that men would do to you, do so to them; for this is the law and the prophets.*"

That which gives the measure of love is Christ in person. Thus, the measure is no longer simply human: it becomes a divine measure. To love as Christ loved is to love in the manner of he who is God and became man.

Like Christ, we train ourselves to be ready, to be generously available, for the supreme sacrifice: *"By this we know love: He gave his life for us; that he laid down his life for us; and we ought to lay down our lives for the brethren."*

Dear brothers and sisters, live without respite in total faithfulness to your consecration, and you will be ready for the sacrifice of love.

GAETA, JUNE 25, 1989

Turn to St. Joseph, you consecrated souls, and you will see reflected in his virginal chastity and spiritual paternity the highest ideals of your vocation. He teaches you love for meditation and prayer, generous fidelity to the commitments assumed before God and the Church, disinterested dedication to the Community in which Providence has placed you, however small and neglected it is. In the light of his example you can learn to appreciate the value of that which is humble, simple, and hidden, of that which is accomplished without conspicuous display or sensationalism but with decisive effects, in the unfathomable depths of the heart.

TERMOLI, MARCH 19, 1983

Love for the Church

"If you keep my commandments, you will abide in my love." Faith is the proof of love. In addition, Christians have the right to require of a consecrated person sincere adherence and obedience to the commandments of Christ and his Church. Therefore, you must avoid everything that might make people think that the Church maintains a dual hierarchy or a dual Magisterium.* Always live and instill profound love for the Church, and loyal adherence to all its teachings. Convey certainties of faith, not uncertainties. Always communicate the truths that the Magisterium states, not ideologies that come and go. To build up the Church, live holiness. It will lead you, if necessary, to the supreme test of love for others, because *"greater love has no man than this, that a man lay down his life for his friends."*

Along these lines, I wish to express all my respect and encouragement for the members of Secular Institutes and Associations of Apostolic Life, who work actively and give testimony of Christ, by their special presence, in all areas of Church life.

PERU, FEBRUARY 1, 1985

---

* The Magisterium is the teaching office of the Church, whose task it is to give an authentic interpretation of the word of God, whether in its written form or in the form of tradition.

Christians have the right to require
of a consecrated person
that he love the Church,
defend it,
fortify and enrich it
by his adherence and obedience.
This faith
must be not merely external
but principally interior,
profound, joyful, and offered in sacrifice.
You must avoid everything that
might make the faithful think
that there exists in the Church
a dual Magisterium,
the authentic one of the Church
and that of theologians and thinkers,
or that the standards of the Church
have today lost their value.

MADRID, NOVEMBER 2, 1982

Faith in Christ requires a *triple faithfulness:*
faithfulness to the Gospel,
faithfulness to the Church,
faithfulness to the particular charism
of your institute.

You must be faithful to the Gospel above all. Your first commitment is to listen to the word of God, pondering it in your heart and attempting to put it into practice. Try to find time every day to meditate on the word of God, trusting in its capacity to enlighten you and lead you to live in the spirit of the beatitudes.

In the second place, your *religious consecration,* besides reinforcing your devotion to Christ, *also binds you inseparably to the life and holiness of his Bride, the Church.* This takes on concrete expression in the local ecclesial community. Thus it is very important for you to work in close collaboration with the clergy and the laity of the local Church, willingly accepting the authority and ministry of the local bishop as the center of that unity.

Finally, *always be faithful to the particular charism of your specific institute.*

PHILIPPINES, FEBRUARY 17, 1981

I wish to emphasize *loving docility to the Magisterium of the Church,* which is a natural consequence of your special ecclesial position. As you know, the religious life has no meaning except in the Church and in fidelity to her directives. "*It would be a serious error to render independent—and even more serious to oppose to each other—the religious life and ecclesial structures, as if they could subsist as two distinct realities, the one charismatic, the other institutional. The two elements, that is, spiritual gifts and ecclesial structures, form a single if complex reality.*" I therefore urge you to be always ready to welcome the teaching of the Church and to contribute—while being faithful to your charism—to the pastoral activity of your local dioceses, under the direction of your bishops, joined with Peter and in union with Christ. Your adherence to the word of God as it is proclaimed by the Church will be the measure of your success in communicating the truth and freedom of Christ. The Holy Spirit, which makes us attentive to "signs of the times," has endowed the Church of Christ with the apostolic and pastoral charism of the Magisterium, in a manner that can effectively hand on Christ's life-giving and liberating word of truth. Let us always remember Jesus' words: "*You will know the truth and the truth will make you free.*"

PHILIPPINES, FEBRUARY 17, 1981

Dear brothers and sisters! You must share in the responsibility for the future of our Church. You yourselves must be the Church. In your associations you bear witness to the fundamental attributes of the Church, of the unique, holy, Catholic, and apostolic Church.

Be a single thing among yourselves, the pillars and props of unity among Christ's flock and its shepherds, sent by Christ. Do not be concerned about prestige, about self, about pride, but be "a heart and a soul." Vigorously promote the unity of divided Christianity!

Be holy! Yes, sanctify your lives and fill your minds only with what is holy. Only when your own life takes on the immutable attributes of the Gospel will you succeed in making men marvel, and drawing them in. And, in your testimony to the world, you serve the sanctification of the world.

Be Catholic, universal, open, worldly. Do not shut yourselves up in your worries and your problems. Your contribution is needed for all humanity, for the Third World, for Europe, so that there can be a new beginning.

Finally, be apostles, witnesses of faith in accord with the Pope and the bishops, and at the same time courageous in your irreplaceable and indispensable commitment.

GERMANY, NOVEMBER 18, 1980

The Church needs lay Christian saints

Yes, it needs saints, more than reformers, because saints are the most authentic and productive reformers. Every great period of renewal in the Church is linked to important testimonials of holiness. Without such testimonials the updating undertaken by the Councils would be illusive.

But the conviction that we must share and spread this call to holiness is addressed to all Christians. This call is not the privilege of a spiritual élite. Nor is it for a few who feel heroic courage. Still less is it a tranquil refuge, suited to a certain type of piety or to certain eccentric temperaments. It is a grace offered to all the baptized, in varying forms and degrees.

It is not reserved for particular states of life, although some favor it, or for the practice of certain professions. St. Francis of Sales showed effectively that holiness, with piety or devotion, could be an attribute of men and women in any family situation or career. Thus lay people must be encouraged to live every aspect of their life in the world—whatever the specific circumstances in which God has placed them—in a holy manner, in faith, hope, and love. In this sense, there is a kind of holiness specific to lay people.

JUNE 7, 1986

The Apostolate

The world wants to see Jesus in you

The man of today looks at you and repeats what the Greek visitors to Jerusalem said to the Apostle Philip: *"We wish to see Jesus." Yes, in you the world wishes to see Jesus.* Your public declaration of the evangelical principles is a radical response to God's call to follow him. As a result your life aims at offering clear testimony to the reality of the Kingdom of God already present in the activities of men and nations.

Many know what you do and admire and value you for it. But your true greatness comes from what you are. Perhaps what you are is less well known and understood. In fact, what you are can be understood only in the light of the "newness of life" revealed by Christ Resurrected. In Christ you are a "new creation."

GREAT BRITAIN, MAY 29, 1982

A bridge between the Church and the world

Even today the Church is not tired of giving the gift of God's mercy. At the same time, it strives tirelessly to make the barren earth fertile. You can help the Church accomplish that by the contribution you make in your particular lay mission. The laity is both a sign of salvation *in the world and a bridge between the Church and the world.* Often you are in much closer contact than priests and religious with the conditions of life, the needs, the hopes, and the spiritual contradictions of our time. Only with a generous Apostolate of lay people, united with the pastors of the Church and given life by sacramental Grace, is the Church truly the Church.

SEPTEMBER 12, 1983

Here is the style of the evangelical worker: It is the way he goes courageously along the paths of the world, utterly detached from the things of the earth, bringing peace and proclaiming the coming of the Kingdom. Today, even more than in the past, he goes announcing to mankind the good news of God's merciful love and, with it, the duty to respond to this pre-existing love; as he goes he must promote the integral good of men; as he goes he must be careful not to set the commitments of service to God and service to one's brothers against each other but, instead, coordinate in a balanced synthesis the so-called vertical dimension, which extends on high, toward God, and the horizontal, which moves in the direction of men.

ASSISI, MARCH 12, 1982

Dear sisters and brothers, today, as in the time of St. Benedict, and even more, the Church counts heavily on you and your collaboration. As you well know, the task of evangelization belongs not only to priests but also, in different ways, to all the faithful, because they, too, are moved by the Holy Spirit to bear witness to Christ and his Gospel.

The Church relies on you today more than ever, not only because it reads in your souls the vocation to a full Christian life but also because it recognizes the great possibilities in what you can contribute to the formation and coordination of the various diocesan ecclesial movements. You must know how to take up your responsibilities with optimism, looking realistically at the present and hopefully to the future. Above all, you must know how to conquer indifference, inertia, and every other obstacle with the light of faith and the energy of love. Thus you will see your organizations flourish, and give glory to God and joy to your brothers.

SEPTEMBER 20, 1980

The second condition is that, in terms of knowledge and experience, you must be truly *competent in your specific field,* in order to carry out, through your presence, the Apostolate of witness and commitment to others that your consecration and your life in the Church impose on you. In fact, it is solely thanks to this competence that you can put into practice the recommendation that the Council made to the members of Secular Institutes: *"They must endeavor first of all to give themselves entirely to God, in perfect charity, and their institutes must preserve their secular character, especially and specifically for the purpose of practicing everywhere and effectively the apostolate for which they were created."*

AUGUST 28, 1980

You are called on to take up your role in the evangelization of the world. Yes, the laity are *"a chosen people, a holy priesthood."* They are called on to be *"the salt of the earth"* and *"the light of the world."* It is their vocation and their unique mission to manifest the Gospel in their lives and also to add it as leaven to the world in which they live and work. The great forces that rule the world—politics, mass media, science, technology, culture, education, industry, and work—represent precisely the areas in which lay people are competent to carry out their mission. If these forces are controlled by people who are true disciples of Christ and whose knowledge and talents make them, at the same time, experts in their particular field, then the world will truly be changed from within by the redeeming power of Christ.

AUGUST 28, 1980

The people value your presence and the pastors consider it a "gift" from the Lord. Living in fraternity and sharing the sufferings and joys of the "humblest," you proclaim by your actions that the heavenly Father never forgets the various stages of human existence. Your role is truly singular: *You make the Church present in the most complex and delicate situations;* you bring the warmth of God's love to those who feel alone and without affection. *You offer,* in short, *the living proof that God loves every person, especially the weakest and most defenseless.*

In this region, tested by nature and still marked by the memory of the recent earthquake, your work is both providential and a bonus. You are the living voice of the Gospel, serving the humble and the lowest, whom the Lord prefers! You glorify the Savior in freely consecrating yourselves to serve them, listening to their demands, seeking with the means at your disposal to meet their needs, but above all offering them the light of faith, which opens them to trust and to the transcendent dimension of life. Be prepared in any situation *"to make a defense to any one who calls you to account for the hope that is in you."*

POTENZA, APRIL 28, 1991

You must be available and competent to meet the spiritual needs, and often the material needs as well, of your brothers and sisters: from helping in the parish to catechizing children, from staffing centers for children from troubled families to working in hospitals and nursing homes, nursery schools and old people's homes. Many of you, besides, are employed directly in government social services or public assistance programs, especially for the sick.

All of that, though demanding and difficult, cannot but fill your hearts with joy and make you value the singular gift of the consecrated life. Choosing to serve the poorest, you write pages of hope every day in what are certainly marginal areas and, firmly integrated into the diocesan pastoral work, you effectively proclaim the Gospel of mercy and fraternity.

POTENZA, APRIL 28, 1991

You who belong to Secular Institutes, committed to keeping the lamp of faith and Christian charity lighted and shining in the world, have the important yet delicate charge of educating souls in the doctrine, piety, and discipline that characterize the followers of the Divine Redeemer. In fact, the Church has the unique mission of continuing in the present the Revelation and the Redemption of Christ.

You must therefore have an abundance of inner fervor, so that you may be able to give to others, communicate the joy of the Truth, and be an instrument of "grace." From this flows the exhortation to be faithful to an intense inner life, nourished above all by celebration of the Holy Mass, by Eucharistic devotion, and by daily meditation. Only through the Eucharist is it possible to maintain the innocence of children, the purity of young people, matrimonial chastity and fidelity.

PRATO, MARCH 19, 1986

I now direct my words to you members of Secular Institutes. I know the great contribution you make and can make, through your joyful testimony and your apostolic action, fortified by constant prayer. Now I would like to make a recommendation that is especially close to my heart:

Courageously proclaim Christ who calls; for he continues to call today, as he did yesterday, and he uses us as the means to make his appeals heard.

Therefore proclaim him in Christian communities, proclaim him with particular force to young people.

In many places there are young people of a new type growing up, who are open to the life of the Church and society.

Do not disappoint their expectations. Be, then, messengers of the will of God and call with courage!

Message for the World Day of Prayer
for Vocations, 1984

Testimony

You must not forget that the *testimony of your life* is extremely important in a society besieged by the temptation to turn values upside down and strive for personal security and well-being above all: always wanting to have more. You must bear witness to the evangelical values that can save man's complete integrity. The testimony of your life as you follow Christ chaste, poor, and obedient highlights the false security of the goods of this world, when they are valued above the true good of the person and the community.

In the light of Christ who is the way, the truth, and the life, it seems clear that man *"cannot find himself fully except through the sincere gift of himself."* In the context of the evangelical doctrine that you bear witness to, we can understand why *"man is more valuable for what he is than for what he has."* For this reason, true wealth consists not in having, and not even in giving, but in the capacity to give oneself and, hence, share life with your brothers and sisters who are suffering and seek the truth. Your chastity, poverty, and obedience are a sign of Jesus' love: living the destiny of your brothers and sisters in solidarity, giving yourself, not belonging to yourself, following the Father's universal plan of salvation. You, and your life, are *"a sign and stimulus of charity and a special source of spiritual fecundity in the world."*

BOLIVIA, MAY 10, 1988

You are called to evangelize first of all with your life. The renewal of faith begins with the identification of the message with the messenger.

Therefore be witnesses of the Gospel with your entire, committed, exemplary life, so that the faithful can always recognize you, even from the outside. Be transparent, so that the evangelical counsels, the charism of your founders, fraternal communion in a simple, pure life are visible in you. You, members of the Secular Institutes, must bring to society, by your lay state, Christ's presence among men, with testimony that questions those who live with you and compels them to question themselves.

Over all, in the tasks of evangelization and catechism that belong to the ecclesial plan, I ask that you show special devotion to young people in the parish communities, the Catholic schools, groups and associations, the ecclesial spiritual movements. And you must also devote yourselves to the integral formation of committed lay people in the Church and in society.

VENEZUELA, JANUARY 28, 1985

You live in the service of love. You are servants of love for love of Christ. In this way you achieve the maturity of human beings who offer God their own freedom and use it in his service. Therefore, every day meditate on and renew the reasons of faith that motivate and sustain your life, your devotion, and your faithfulness, which is joyous and fruitful, though offered in sacrifice. And when you confirm in the silence of prayer—*which is indispensable for you*—the full validity of your life, thank the Lord for his marvels. Proclaim by your holiness that his name is holy.

Christ calls you to be his faithful witness, to be the channel of his saving love in today's world, to spread his mercy, which extends from generation to generation among those who fear him. Hence the shared concrete task of your service is to fulfill the divine plan of salvation: to make present the Kingdom of God, which is the Church; to make it present in your life and your environment, in the school, in the family, among the young, in service to the sick and abandoned, in charitable institutions, in works of social benefit, and, above all, in parish and catechetical initiatives, in order to bring to all the love of Christ and through him love for mankind. And do not forget the influential world of culture, which is vital for evangelization and the creation of a just social system. Thus the Gospel will be incarnate in the life and culture of your people, affecting the various social classes and promoting true human and Christian values.

VENEZUELA, JANUARY 28, 1985

And you, who are consecrated to God as members of Secular Institutes, will give illuminating testimony through your apostolic work, which will lead every temporal reality to God.

CHILE, APRIL 1, 1987

Be witnesses!

I would like to urge you today: *Be witnesses.* Witnesses of the hope that is rooted in faith. Witnesses of the invisible in a secularized society, which too often ignores every transcendent dimension.

Yes, consecrated souls: among the people of this generation, who are so immersed in the *relative,* you must be voices that speak of the *absolute.* Perhaps you have, so to speak, thrown all your resources into the scales of the world, gladly tipping them toward God and the goods promised by him? You have made a decisive choice about your life: you have opted for generosity and giving in the face of greed and self-interest; you have chosen to count on love and grace, challenging those who consider you ingenuous and ineffectual; you have placed every hope on the Kingdom of Heaven, when many around you are striving only to assure for themselves a comfortable stay on earth.

It is up to you, now, to *be integrated,* in spite of every difficulty. The spiritual destiny of many souls is linked to your faith and your integration.

You must be the constant reminder of that destiny which unfolds in time but has eternity as its goal, bearing witness with your words, and even more with your lives, that we must of necessity direct ourselves toward the one who is the inescapable end point of the parabola of our existence.

Your vocation
makes you the advance guard
of mankind on the march:
in your prayers
and in your work,
in your joy
and in your suffering,
in your successes
and in your trials,
mankind must be able to find
the model and the future
of what it, too,
is called to be,
in spite of its own burdens
and its own compromises.

BOLOGNA, APRIL 18, 1982

The world needs your testimony

The world today needs to see your love for Christ; it needs public testimony of the religious life: as Paul VI once said: "*Modern man listens more willingly to witnesses than to teachers, and if he listens to teachers he does so because they are witnesses.*" If the nonbelievers of this world are to believe in Christ, they need your faithful testimony—testimony that springs from your complete trust in the generous mercy of the Father and in your enduring faith in the power of the cross and the resurrection. Thus the ideals, the values, the convictions that are the basis of your dedication to Christ must be translated into the language of daily life. Among the people of God, in the local ecclesial community, your public testimony is part of your contribution to the mission of the Church. As St. Paul says: "*You are a letter from Christ... written not with ink but with the Spirit of the living God, not on tablets of stone but on tablets of human hearts.*"

PHILIPPINES, FEBRUARY 17, 1981

First, it is your duty to *bear witness.* Because you have been baptized, you must be a sign and instrument of union with God and salvation for the world. The first thing is to live life in the Spirit, by listening to the word, by inner prayer, by the faithful completion of the task assigned to you and the gift of yourself in this service, and by the humility of repentance. On account of your *religious consecration,* you are, for the world, a visible witness of the profound mystery of Christ, because you represent him *"either while he is in contemplation on the mountain, or announces the Kingdom of God to the multitudes, or heals the sick and the wounded and converts sinners to a better life, or blesses the children and does good to all; and he is always obedient to the will of the Father who sent him."* Through your particular vocation, you are a special sign of holiness and apostolic work, and this confers on you a special role in the Church, a role with its own distinctive character. You will always be faithful to this vocation, in spite of temptations. Find happiness in preserving your inner identity and in being recognized for what you are.

PHILIPPINES, FEBRUARY 17, 1981

I am eager to emphasize the "complementariness" between your testimony and that of the "secular" lay faithful. In fact, the testimony of lay people, who live in the world, can be useful in reminding you that consecration must not make you indifferent to the salvation of men or to earthly progress, which is itself willed by God. On the other hand, reciprocally, your testimony can profitably remind committed lay people in the world that earthly progress is not an end in itself.

This places you, if you will allow me the expression, at the "junction" between human and ecclesial reality, between the kingdom of man and the Kingdom of God: with your physical tasks, which shape the proper course of the entire community, and with your presence in the world of school and work—professional, technological—you are called to serve as a connection that leads to a fuller organic unity in that external world, and you can play an extremely important role in encouraging its components to draw closer to the Church.

JANUARY 12, 1980

In every moment of your life and in all your daily activities you must demonstrate "*total availability to the will of the Father, who has placed you in the world and for the world.*" And this means that as members of Secular Institutes you must pay particular attention to three elements that converge in your particular vocation.

The first element has to do with following Christ more nearly on the path of the evangelical counsels, giving yourself completely to the person of the Savior to share his life and mission. This giving, which the Church recognizes as a special consecration, also becomes a challenge to human certainties when they are the fruit of pride. More explicitly, it means the "new world" willed by God and inaugurated by Jesus.

The second element is competence in your specific field, however modest and mundane, with "*full awareness of your part in the enlightenment of society.*" This is necessary so that you may "*serve your brothers with greater generosity and efficacy.*" Thus your testimony will be more credible.

The third element has to do with a transforming presence in the world, which means making "*a personal contribution to the realization of God's providential plan in history,*" animating, with the evangelical spirit, the order of temporal realities, and perfecting them, by acting from within those very realities.

AUGUST 28, 1984

Without Christ everything is too little

May the heart of each of you, who have given up earthly paternity and maternity, be always overflowing with the inestimable treasure of spiritual paternity and maternity, which so many of your brothers are in urgent need of! You do not love less; you love more!

Why is your service so highly valued? Not only because of your particular ability, not only because with your way of life you can give more time; but mainly because men perceive that through you works an other. In fact, to the extent to which you live your full dedication, you live in him; and ultimately he claims the human heart.

GERMANY, NOVEMBER 18, 1980

Taking an interest in the world in order to transform it

Christians, and especially you members of the laity, are called by God to become interested in the world in order to transform it according to the Gospel. Your personal commitment to truth and honesty occupies an important position in the fulfillment of that task, because a sense of responsibility to truth constitutes one of the fundamental meeting points between the Church and society, between the Church and each man or woman. The Christian faith does not provide ready-made solutions to the complex problems of contemporary society, but it does provide a deep understanding of human nature and its needs, calling you to tell the truth in charity, to take up your responsibilities as good citizens, and to work, along with your neighbor, to construct a society in which genuine human values are fostered and intensified through a shared Christian vision of life.

NAIROBI, MAY 7, 1980

We have to be for others

Our times require mature and balanced personalities.

Ideological confusion produces psychologically immature and needy personalities; pedagogy itself wavers and sometimes goes astray. For this very reason, the modern world searches anxiously for models, and most of the time remains disappointed, defeated, humiliated. That is why we have to develop mature personalities, which means learning to keep our selfishness in check, assuming our proper roles of responsibility and leadership, and trying to fulfill ourselves wherever we are and in whatever work we do.

Our times require serenity and courage to accept reality as it is, without discouraging criticisms or utopian fantasies, to love it and to save it.

All of you, then, undertake to reach these ideals of "maturity," through love of duty, meditation, spiritual reading, examination of your conscience, spiritual guidance, and regular use of the Sacrament of Repentance. The Church and modern society need mature personalities: we must fill that need, with the help of God!

Finally, our times require a serious commitment to holiness.

The spiritual needs of the present world are immense! It is almost frightening to look at the infinite forests of buildings in a modern metropolis, inhabited by countless numbers of people. How will we be able to reach all these people and lead them to Christ?

The certainty that we are merely instruments of grace comes to our aid: acting in the individual soul is God himself, with his love and mercy.

Our true, lifelong commitment must be to personal sanctification, so that we may be fit and efficacious instruments of grace.

The truest and most sincere wish I have for you is just this: "Become holy and soon be saints!"

ST. PIO V PARISH, OCTOBER 28, 1979

May your life be a light for the world

The words of Jesus are valid for you in a very special way: *"Let your light shine so before men, that they may see your good works and give glory to your Father who is in heaven."* Yes, brothers and sisters! the light of your faith shines bright; the light of your chastity joyfully; the light of your poverty generously!

How much the Church and the world need this light, this testimony! How deeply we must commit ourselves, so that its full splendor and its utter eloquence may be realized!

How essential it is that we reproduce in ourselves, mortal beings, the mystery of Christ's devotion to the Father for the salvation of the world: the miraculous devotion that began with the presentation in the temple, whose memory the whole Church celebrates today.

How essential it is that we, too, fix our gaze on the soul of Mary, on the soul that, according to the words of Simeon, would be pierced by a sword so the thoughts of many hearts might be revealed.

FEBRUARY 2, 1980

Apostolic witness in the spirit of love and service

It is a question of insisting on the need for adult Catholic men to be an active presence in the world, on the need for their Christian testimony and their apostolic action, so that the Church, as the leaven, can penetrate all of human society, structured as it is, and marked by so many ideologies alien to the spirit of the Gospel. On the other hand, how to reach these men, who are often involved in and absorbed by their earthly responsibilities or worries, and neglect or forget the religious dimension of their lives? Is it not through other men, similar to them, who are busy as they are, except that they seek God and worship him unceasingly, and follow and serve Jesus Christ? How can we not hope that everywhere in the world Catholic men of every social condition, with duties and responsibilities at every level, will join apostolic associations, solidly integrated in parishes and cities, and find there the thorough Christian training that will help and prepare them to bring true apostolic testimony, sufficient to the needs of the present moment and animated by a spirit of love, service, and renewal according to the Gospel?

TO THE INTERNATIONAL
FEDERATION OF CATHOLIC MEN,
OCTOBER 28, 1978

If you have met Christ, proclaim it in the first person

If you have met Christ, live Christ, live with Christ! Proclaim it in the first person, as genuine testimony: *"For me life is Christ."* That is true liberation: to proclaim Jesus free of ties, present in men and women, transformed, made new creatures. Why instead at times does our testimony seem to be in vain? Because we present Jesus without the full seductive power of his person, without revealing the treasures of the sublime ideal inherent in following him; and because we are not always successful in demonstrating conviction, translated into living terms, regarding the extraordinary value of the gift of ourselves to the ecclesial cause we serve.

Brothers and sisters: it is important that men see in us dispensers of the mysteries of God, credible witnesses of his presence in the world. We frequently remember that God, when he calls us, asks for not only one part of our person but all our person and all our vital energies, so that we may announce to men the joy and peace of a new life in Christ, and guide them to a meeting with him. So let it be our first concern to seek the Lord, and, once we have met him, to observe where and how he lives, by being with him all day. Being with him, in a special way, in the Eucharist, where Christ gives himself to us; and in prayer, through which we give ourselves to him. The Eucharist must be performed and extended into our daily actions as a "sacrifice of praise." In prayer, in the trusting contact with God our Father, we can discern better where our strengths and weaknesses are, because the Spirit comes to our aid. The same Spirit speaks to us and slowly immerses us in the divine mysteries, in God's design of love for humanity, which he realizes through our willingness to serve him.

JANUARY 26, 1979

Bringing Christ into the world

You call yourselves: Missionaries of the Kingship of Christ. Nothing is more sublime, nothing more essential! To bring Christ into the world; to live the Gospel of Christ, proclaim it to mankind, which is always thirsting for truth, and to bear witness of its force and newness in the world of culture and higher education: this is your ideal and the plan for your life! Be happy to be Missionaries of the King of love and peace, of justice and holiness!

You are well aware of the clinical portrait of society at the end of the twentieth century; you can make a diagnosis of our times.

Despite the formidable advances in science and technology that we all benefit from, there is an alarming feeling of unease and insecurity. Minds are muffled in ideological confusion, and so transcendence is denied, or relegated to a vague, emotional mysticism. Consequently, it is logical to speak of a radical crisis of values, leading, distressingly, to a tense situation of social unrest and pedagogic uncertainty; of impatience, fear, violence, neurosis. In this situation, Jesus says to you, too, as to the Apostles: *"Do not fear those who kill the body"*; *"I am with you always, to the close of the age."*

In a world that is afflicted and tormented by so many doubts and so much anguish, you must be missionaries of certainty:

- certainty concerning transcendent values, reached through the good and healthy philosophy—justly called "everlasting," in the footsteps of St. Thomas Aquinas—but integrated with contributions from modern thought;
- certainty concerning the person of Christ, true man and true God, the historical and definitive manifestation of God to man, for his inward enlightenment and redemption;
- certainty concerning the historical reality and divine mission of the Church, willed expressly by Christ for the transmission of the revealed doctrine and as the means of holiness and salvation.

What an exalting task awaits you in your work, in your professions, in the daily contact with your brothers and sisters! Christ rules in your hearts, in your thoughts, in your seeking, in your preoccupations, in your feelings, so that anyone who meets you can understand how wonderful, great, worthy, joyous to be Christian! And may most holy Mary, Queen of Knowledge, assist you and inspire you, so that you, too, may always magnify the Lord, who has chosen you to be missionaries of truth and love!

To the Missionaries of the
Kingship of Christ,
August 19, 1979

All Christians are called to bear witness and are qualified to do so. With particular urgency those who are bound to the Church not only in their private lives but also in their professional lives are "men and women of the Church." We must all ask ourselves if our testimony concerning our personal lives and our public and professional attitudes corresponds to what men expect from the Church and the Church expects from men.

For many of you the testimony of faith becomes the substance of your profession.

GERMANY, NOVEMBER 18, 1980

I Exhort You

With all my heart I exhort you,
whose religious consecration
should make you even more readily available
for service to the Church,
to prepare as well as possible
for the task of catechesis,
according to the differing vocations
of your institutes
and the missions entrusted to you,
and to carry this concern everywhere.
Let the communities devote
their best abilities
and means
to the specific work of catechesis!

CATECHESI TRADENDAE, 65

Learn how to cultivate a spirituality that, opening itself to perceive God's work in the world, responsibly assumes the task of collaborating in the realization of his designs for salvation. Using all the resources of perception, you must make every effort to grasp the needs of your contemporaries, so that you can try to respond with all the wealth of your heart. It is your duty to commit yourselves to fulfilling all the gifts of your intelligence, so that your service may be more competent and hence more worthy of Jesus, whom you meet in every brother love pushes you toward.

And be happy in the practice of your daily tasks, because it is written that *"God loves those who give joyfully."*

JANUARY 12, 1980

You must be, above all, *true disciples of Christ:* and, as members of a Secular Institute, you want to be, with your radical commitment to follow the evangelical counsels in a way that not only does not change your state—you are and remain lay people!—but reinforces it, in the sense that *your secular state* is sanctified, and more demanding; at the same time, your commitment in the world and for the world, implied by the secular state, is permanent and faithful.

You should be well aware of what this means: the special consecration, which fulfills the commitment of baptism and confirmation, must engage your whole life and all your daily activities, creating in you total availability to the will of the Father who has placed you in the world and for the world. In this way consecration will become the medium of discernment, and you will not run the risk of simply accepting the secular state as such, with a facile optimism, but will be conscious of the permanent ambiguity that accompanies it, and as a result you will feel committed to distinguish its positive and negative elements, in order to strengthen the former—precisely by exercising discernment—and progressively eliminate the others.

AUGUST 28, 1980

I hope from the bottom of my heart that the joint presence of the consecrated and the married in a single Secular Institute may be an incentive for them to proclaim together, according to their respective states, the love of Christ, meaning both virginal and conjugal love.

In particular I urge you to keep on with your immediate commitment to making the sublime ideal of the family, and the responsibilities it entails, understood. Be faithful evangelizers of God's plan concerning marriage and the family, presenting it as it genuinely is and making clear that only if the Gospel is welcomed are the hopes that man legitimately places in matrimony and family fully realized. To that end, I gladly encourage the work carried out in the "schools of family life," especially in the courses of specialized preparation and of spiritual formation for the benefit of engaged and newly married couples.

APRIL 25, 1983

Dear friends, I invite you above all to *give thanks to God*. He offers you an extraordinary gift in calling you to leave everything to follow him and serve him. This call can be heard in many ways: it becomes part of each one's secret history; the Church affirmed it. Preserve the memory of the Lord's blessings, and walk in hope. The gifts of the Lord are without repentance. On this path you, like Christ, like Mary, will obviously find your cross. You suffer because of the obstacles that the Gospel encounters, when your mission is to preach to the world; you suffer also from your labors, your limits, sometimes from your weaknesses. *Be content* to be so close to Christ and so useful to the Church. Even if, often, you cannot visibly check the results of your ministry, rejoice, as Jesus said to his apostles, in the fact that your names are written in Heaven. If you are faithful, you will always find Christ's peace.

You know the path of faith. Put prayer at the center of your lives. Live in close union with Christ. Live with him all the encounters and activities of your apostolate. Remain united among yourselves, so that none of you will lack fraternal support.

BELGIUM, MAY 18, 1985

Dear members of the institutes of special consecration, I would like to confirm you in faithfulness to your particular charism, whose aim, in addition to insuring the effort of evangelical perfection that the Lord has called you to, is to enrich the ecclesial fabric.

Your presence and your participation in pastoral work—which are so much appreciated—are a truly precious, indeed irreplaceable, contribution.

I end with an exhortation that I take from the pastoral heart of Bishop Albino Luciani, Pope John Paul I: be "good samaritans" among the people of God and in society. He was inspired by the parable of the Good Samaritan to a series of spiritual exercises, dense with reflections, which concluded with some hopeful advice: *"If you have a difficult task, do not be demoralized, do not lose courage, never, ever. But with the energy you have received from God, hold fast. Do not trust only in your own strength, but believe that there is also the Lord who helps you, whatever your place."*

Trusting in God and concentrating your energies will perpetually fortify hope, the hope that—as John Paul I declared—is obligatory for every Christian.

So that it may truly be so, I fervently invoke for all of you the most precious heavenly thanks.

VITTORIO VENETO, JUNE 15, 1985

You are consecrated lay people, a large number of collaborators and associates. With your differing charisms you are sent to carry out all the tasks in which the Church's mission is realized. You go to distant places where evangelization is still recent, or you work in countries where Christianity is old but where evangelization must be renewed. You work with young people, the poor, and the sick; you collaborate with pastoral institutions; you bring your testimony to areas where the Christian message is unknown.

Everywhere you go, you go with trust, strong in the provident and inclusive charity inspired by your common Father. You are close to everyone, and you know how to listen attentively to those who are needy or disoriented, those for whom hope seems impossible, for whom peace seems inaccessible. You know how to give fraternal support that helps them go forward in life. You know how to say the word that enlightens because it comes from God with the power of the Spirit of Jesus.

Do not be discouraged in the face of difficulties. Humbly take up your share of the burden of the Church. Lead new workers into the camp of the Gospel.

FRANCE, OCTOBER 7, 1986

Living signs of the Kingdom

You are called to be living signs of the Kingdom! May you therefore be the lamp that gives light, the salt that does not lose its taste. The greater the need to distinguish yourselves clearly in a world that is confused because it lacks high ideals, the greater is your apostolic commitment. The deeper you are inserted into temporal realities, the more clearly you will have to appear in your works as what you are: a herald of the newness of life in Christ. You are called to be signs and, therefore, to respond to the clear and concrete needs in the reality in which you live! If a sign becomes faded, it loses its reason for being, and becomes disorienting and confusing. Only to the extent to which, like the Virgin of Nazareth, you renew your "yes" in every moment of your life, powerfully reinforcing the commitment undertaken with your vows, will you be integrated with the identity you have acquired and personally affirmed in the Church. Your "yes" is united with Mary's "yes." *"This decree of Mary's—'let it be to me'—decided for humankind the fulfillment of the divine mystery."*

PERU, MAY 15, 1988

"*Be of good cheer,*" Jesus says to you, "*I have overcome the world.*"

If Jesus asks you for faith, it is because he gave you faith first. he gave you faith when, with an absolutely free gesture of love, he called you to follow him more nearly, to "*leave house or brothers or sisters or mother or father or lands for my sake and the Gospel.*" He gave you faith when, with a special outpouring of the Spirit, he consecrated you and, amid the diversity of gifts and ministries, "*chose you and appointed you that you should go and bear fruit and that your fruit should abide.*" He gave you faith when he chose you and sent you—you precisely—to be heralds of his Kingdom, witnesses of his Resurrection, a prophetic sign of the "*new heavens and a new earth, in which righteousness dwells.*"

Your mission, like the mission of the entire Church at the end of the second Christian millennium, is not easy.

Jesus did not hide from his Apostles the *difficulties of the mission:* the rejection, the hostility, the persecution they would encounter. "*If the world hates you, know that it has hated me before it hated you. . . . Remember the word that I said to you: A servant is not greater than his master. If they persecuted me, they will persecute you, too.*"

That which might seem an obstacle to your mission becomes, in the light of faith, the secret of its fruitfulness. The presence of the paschal Christ assures us that, just when we seem defeated, then we are the conquerors, in fact "more than conquerors." It is the remarkable logic that flows from the Cross. On the human level, the Cross of Jesus is a notable failure; but from it derives the explosive newness that changed the face of life and human history.

Here is the secret of our faith: when we are weak, it is then that we are strong; and the weaker we are, the stronger we are, because the more we let the presence and the power of the paschal Christ shine through. And with this paradox the Church has walked for two thousand years already and will go on walking . . . nothing else, only this paradox.

The Spirit of God is the Spirit of life, which can make life explode even where everything seemed dead and parched. That is why we can and must have faith. We not only can but must. Hope for Christians, and even more for the consecrated, is not a luxury, it is a duty. To hope is not to dream; on the contrary, it is to let oneself by seized by he who can transform the dream into reality.

REGGIO EMILIA, JUNE 6, 1988

Strive to be witnesses of Christ's love by putting into practice his Word of Life.

When you help your neighbor, whoever he is, you proclaim the Good News of Christ, which makes universal brotherhood possible.

When you visit a sick person, you are a sign of Christ's mercy toward those who suffer.

When you forgive, even your worst enemy, you are a sign of the forgiveness of Christ, who never nourished hatred in his heart.

When you refuse to accuse someone without proof, you proclaim the coming of the Kingdom of God and his justice, and no one is excluded.

When, as Christian spouses, you remain faithful in marriage, you are an encouragement to all and a sign of the eternal covenant of love between God and man.

When, as a young man or a young woman, you save yourself for the one who will be your spouse, you are testimony of the unique value that love can construct.

When you radiate Christ, you awaken a desire for total self-giving in his service and inspire new priestly and religious vocations.

When, in the light, you call evil that which is evil and refuse to practice it, you are witnesses of Christ's Light.

May our Lord of Peace help you to be, for your brothers and sisters, men and women of light, authors of peace and reconciliation who can be builders of a more just and fraternal world.

CHAD, JUNE 30, 1990

The Son of God, *poor for the sake of love,* became the servant of every human being, especially of the defenseless and the humble.

Walk unhesitatingly in the wake of the evangelical predilection for the weak, the poor. And without reducing your apostolate to pure social action, make yourselves defenders of justice, promoters of genuine Christian fraternity. Be *brothers and sisters of those who have no hope,* of those who aspire to true liberty, of those who seek God. *Be defenders of man and of life,* always ready to meet any form of material or spiritual need. The secret of your mission—as you well know—lies in your *remaining profoundly rooted in supernatural love.* For this reason, cherish your day of prayer: do not forgo the *intimate and transforming union* with the Lord. The soul finds refreshment in prolonged personal contact with him, and the missionary commitment gains renewed strength every day.

May the Lord grant your institutes the gift of many holy vocations and make your precious service to the Church and to humanity productive. May he give comfort to your efforts and your labors.

May the Holy Virgin, *Virgo fidelis,* the outstanding model for the consecrated life, help you and protect you always.

MAY 25, 1991

You must be *the sign and leaven of brotherhood*. God wishes to build in the world the great family of God, where all men, of every race, color and condition, can live together in a spirit of fellowship and peace. You are already a wonderful manifestation of this family. Therefore you can help your people establish themselves as a people-family, from different families and cultures. . . .

Finally, you must be *the sign and leaven of the liberating and saving Love of God for your people and for all men.* Consecrated love originates in the Holy Spirit, but as a response to situations and needs in the Church and in men. God is the Savior and does not want anyone to be lost.

All those who approach you would like to see the face of Christ the Redeemer, *"who desires all men to be saved and to come to the knowledge of the truth."* Be witnesses of God in your way of life and prayer, open up *"the immense spaces of charity, of the evangelical proclamation, of Christian education, of culture, and of solidarity with the poor, the discriminated against, the marginalized, and the oppressed."* Be the vehicle of liberating hope for those who suffer because of slavery, and lead your brothers and sisters to the Sacrament of divine Mercy, of Reconciliation.

Be a sign of God. You must be his witnesses: he is the center and the source of life for mankind.

ANGOLA, JUNE 9, 1992

Everything is a gift

Dear *consecrated lay people,* a special mission in the Church is entrusted to you, too: to be *the voice that denounces enslavement to every form of materialism,* and that through the testimony of chastity, poverty, and obedience—the expression of evangelical radicalism—anticipates, and recalls to the men and women of today, the vitality of the Word of Jesus: *"Blessed are those who have not seen and yet have believed."* Here is the surprising *"news"* that your presence inserts in the din of so many noises and so many deafening voices in the world!

Dear brothers and sisters! May you never forget that *everything is a gift of your existence.* Salvation comes from on high: *"The day shall dawn upon us from on high."*

CREMA, JUNE 20, 1992

The Church would like to thank the Most Holy Trinity for the "mystery of woman," and, for every woman—for what constitutes the eternal measure of her feminine dignity, for the "great works of God" which throughout human history have been accomplished in her and through her. After all, wasn't the greatest event in human history—the incarnation of God himself—accomplished in her and through her?

The Church, therefore, *gives thanks for each and every woman:* for mothers, for sisters, for wives; for women consecrated to God in virginity; for women dedicated to the many human beings who await the freely given love of another person; for women who watch over the human beings in the family, which is the fundamental sign of the human community; for women who work professionally, and who are at times burdened by a great social responsibility; for *"perfect"* women and for "weak" women—for all women as they have come forth from the heart of God in all the beauty and richness of their femininity; as they have been embraced by his eternal love; as, together with men, they are pilgrims on this earth, which is the temporal "homeland" of mankind and is sometimes transformed into a "vale of tears"; as they take on, together with men, a common responsibility for the destiny of humanity, according to daily necessities and according to that definitive destiny which the human family has in God himself, in the bosom of the ineffable Trinity.

The Church gives thanks *for all the manifestations of feminine "genius"* that have appeared in the course of history, amid all peoples and nations; she gives thanks for all the charisms that the Holy Spirit has distributed to women in the history of the people of God, for all the victories that the Church owes to their faith, hope, and charity: she gives thanks for all the fruits of feminine holiness.

The Church asks, at the same time, that these invaluable "manifestations of the Spirit" which are generously poured forth on the "daughters" of eternal Jerusalem be attentively recognized and appreciated, so that they may return to the common benefit of the Church and humanity, especially in our times. Pondering the Biblical mystery of "woman," the Church prays that all women may discover in this mystery themselves and their "supreme vocation."

MULIERIS DIGNITATEM, 31

Challenge the Young

Challenge young
people to follow Christ

May I ask of you one thing?
You are surely aware
of the needs of the Church
in every part of the world
regarding the call
to the priesthood and the religious life.
My request is that you
never fail
to challenge the young
to follow Christ
on this path.
Help them discover
the divine call.
Sustain them with your prayers,
your counsel,
and with the example of your lives.

APRIL 12, 1984

Give thanks to the Lord for your marvelous vocation. Through you Jesus wants to continue the Sermon on the Mount. He wants to see the Kingdom of God proclaimed, heal the sick, convert sinners, bless children, work for the good of all people, and always obey the will of the Father who sent him. In you the Church and the world must be able to see the living God.

Do not be afraid to proclaim openly before the rest of the Church, especially before young people, the validity and beauty of your way of life. The great honor of following the call of Christ to the religious life must be revealed to the Catholic community. The young must know you more intimately. They will come to you if they see you as generous and joyful followers of Jesus Christ, whose life does not offer material rewards and does not adapt to fit worldly models. They will be attracted by the exalting and uncompromising challenge of Christ to leave everything and follow him.

GREAT BRITAIN, MAY 29, 1982

142

Concrete service to building ecclesial unity will be the best and most effective way of *presenting yourselves to new generations* eager for integrated testimony and proposals that give real meaning to the most vital aspirations of their hearts.

You must therefore help adolescents discover, through appropriate formative programs, the new and different perspective of a *freedom* called to *love* in *truth*. You must yourselves be the living sign that true happiness consists in responding to the divine call and giving yourselves without reserve to God and to your brothers and sisters.

In particular, your primary commitment must be to identify and promote priestly and religious vocations.

TRIESTE, MAY 1, 1992

143

The young people who knock at your door wish to find an ecclesial life that is characterized by *fervent prayer*, by the *spirit of family*, by *apostolic commitment*. These young people are sensitive to the values of community and expect to find them in the religious life. You must be able to welcome them and guide them, carefully cultivating new vocations; looking for these must be one of your principal occupations.

GUATEMALA, MARCH 7, 1983

I am here to remember the numerous *groups, movements, and associations of lay faithful* which the Holy Spirit initiates and fosters in the Church with a view to a more missionary Christian presence in the world. These various groups of lay people are proving to be a particularly fertile field for the manifestation of vocations to consecrated life, truly places where vocations can be encouraged and can grow. Quite a few young people, in fact, in and through these groups. have heard the Lord's call to follow him on the path of the priestly ministry and have responded with heartening generosity. These groups should be utilized well, so that, in communion with the whole Church and for the sake of her growth, they may make their proper contributions to the development of the pastoral work of promoting vocations.

The various elements and members of the Church engaged in the pastoral work of promoting vocations will be more effective in their task the more they stimulate the ecclesial community as such, beginning with the parish, to feel that the problem of priestly vocations cannot simply be delegated to some "official" group (priests in general, priests working in the seminary in particular), because it is "*a vital problem that lies at the very heart of the Church*," and so it should be at the heart of the love that each Christian feels for the Church.

PASTORES DABO VOBIS, 41

Jesus also needs young men who, among you, will follow his call and live like him, in poverty and chastity, so that they may be the living sign of the reality of God in the midst of your brothers and sisters.

God needs priests who will be guided by the good shepherd in the service of his word and his Sacraments for mankind.

He needs religious, both men and women, who will leave everything to follow him and serve humanity.

He needs Christian husbands and wives, who together and with their children will do their best for the full maturation of humanity in God.

God needs men and women who are ready to help the poor, the sick, the rejected, the marginalized, and those whose souls are in pain.

GERMANY, NOVEMBER 19, 1980

To you I say: *Always seek the truth, which makes you free: "Freedom that refuses to be bound to the truth will fall into arbitrariness and end up submitting itself to the vilest of passions, to the point of self-destruction."*

The secret of the attraction and the rapture that Christ, the eternal Youth of history, radiates lies in his perfect communion with the Father and in the total offering up of his life for the work planned by the Father, always doing *"what is pleasing to him."*

You, too, must continually make your existence new and joyous, by uniting it intimately with that of Jesùs. Like him, know that you are available to others, ready and generous. *There is no work more beautiful or greater than to be useful to others for the sake of love.* Neither violence, which destroys everything, nor intolerance, which denies a person's identity, can build anything serious or lasting: only solidarity can, guided and sustained by the force of love, which generates, promotes, and renews everything.

Through your commitment in associations, in movements, in pastoral organizations, be the living and prophetic part of your ecclesial community. Bring hope, bring joy in the new life that alone can satisfy men's hearts.

CASERTA, MAY 24, 1992

Prayer

A constant danger for apostolic workers is to become so involved in their activity for the Lord that they forget that the Lord is in every activity.

They must be aware, therefore, of the ever-increasing importance of prayer in their lives and must learn to devote themselves to it generously. To accomplish that, they need silence in their entire being, which requires regular periods of silence and personal discipline to encourage contact with God.

MARCH 7, 1980

Being with Jesus

How is it possible for a consecrated person, fully taken up with apostolic activity, to grow in his inner life without equal periods of prayer and worship?

Silence is vital space devoted to the Lord, in an atmosphere of listening to his word and assimilating it; it is a sanctuary of prayer, the hearth of reflection and contemplation. To remain fervent and zealous in one's ministry, one must be able to receive divine inspiration from within. And that is possible only if one is capable of *being* with the divine Teacher. Jesus did not call the Twelve only to "*send them forth to preach and to have power to heal sicknesses and to cast out devils*" but, above all, so that "*they should be with him.*"

Being with Jesus: let this be your greatest desire. Be with him as the Apostles were and, earlier, in Nazareth, Mary and Joseph. Speak to him in an intimate way, listen to him, and follow him docilely: this is not only a comprehensible requirement for those who want to follow the Lord; it is also an indispensable condition of all authentic and credible evangelization. He is an empty preacher of the Word—St. Augustine aptly observes—who does not first listen to it within himself.

Be united with Christ forever. The methods that the millenarian wisdom of the Church is never tired of recommending to the faithful, so that they may be disposed to supernatural grace—frequent practice of the Sacrament of Repentance, devout participation in the Holy Mass, celebration of the Liturgy of the Hours, the *Lectio Divina,* Eucharistic worship, the Spiritual Exercises, reciting the Rosary—should be sought and cherished by you, dear brothers and sisters, with even more reason, for you are more closely united with the mission of the Redeemer.

Before being organizers of your communities, be models of prayer and spiritual perfection for them. By constant recourse to prayer you will be able to draw on the inner strength necessary to overcome difficulties, conquer temptations, and grow in charity and fidelity to your vocation.

SORRENTO, MARCH 19, 1992

The soul that lives habitually in the presence of God and is filled with the warmth of his charity will easily avoid the temptation to biases and conflicts that carry the risk of divisiveness; he will be able to interpret in the light of the Gospel the option for the poor and for victims of injustice without yielding to sociopolitical radicalism, which, sooner or later, produces effects opposite to the ones it hopes for and generates new forms of oppression. Finally, the soul that is in contact with God will find the most suitable way to approach people and enter their world without compromising his religious identity, or hiding or masking the specific originality of his vocation, which is following Christ, poor, chaste, and obedient.

MAY 13, 1983

You have felt an urgent need to encounter the Absolute, and so you have discovered the importance of inwardness, of silence, of meditation, in enabling one to grasp a definitive, reconciling sense of existence. You have tasted the sweetness of prayer and of the constantly renewed, enduring reconciliation of friendship with the Lord, fixed in your hearts by an existential attitude of humble and industrious obedience to the Heavenly Father. With St. Benedict, then, I will address to you the eternal invitation: *"Ausculta, O fili, verba magistri"*: Listen, O my child, to the teachings of the master, and make your hearts attentive in the silence of prayer, to return, through the effort of docile obedience to the sound precepts, to him, from whom denial or rebellion has distanced us. Present yourselves often before the inner Teacher, and those who represent him, in the attitude of a true disciple, who knows how to be silent and how to listen.

MARCH 23, 1980

Unity of prayer and action

All of you, through the different kinds of spirituality that animate you, constituting a rich spiritual patrimony for the Church and for humanity, seek to live an authentically Christian and therefore evangelical life by being, as lay people and Christians, "in the world" without being "of the world."

For you lay people, apostolic life requires effective openings for the various means you have of making the evangelical "leaven" penetrate. It involves activities and responsibilities in all areas of human existence: family, professional, social, cultural, political. And it is by taking on these responsibilities competently and in profound union with God that you respond to your vocation as lay people and Christians: that you sanctify yourselves and sanctify the world.

To remain united with God in carrying out your responsibilities is a vital necessity for bearing witness to his love. And only a life based on the sacraments, together with a life of prayer, can increase this intimacy with the Lord.

Taking the time to pray, and to foster prayer and its activities with Bible, theological, and doctrinal studies; to experience Christ and his grace through regular attendance at the Sacraments of Reconciliation and the Eucharist—these are the fundamental requirements of every profoundly Christian life. And thus the Holy Spirit will be the source of both your action and your contemplation, which will then interpenetrate, sustaining each other and bearing much fruit.

This profound unity of prayer and action is the basis of all spiritual renewal, especially among lay people. It is the basis of evangelization and the great work of building up the world according to God's plan. It must be the foundation of the life of our movements and their methods of formation with a view to evangelization.

TO THE GATHERING OF LAY SPIRITUAL MOVEMENTS,
APRIL 18, 1980

It is vital for everyone to recognize the need for prayer and, indeed, to pray, but religious, as people called to be experts in prayer, must seek God and love him above everything; in all circumstances they must try to live a hidden life with Christ in God, a life from which love for one's neighbor flows and becomes a pressing need. Thus you must, for Christ, with Christ, and in Christ, deepen your knowledge, both personal and in the community, of the principal source of apostolic and charitable activity; in that way, you will participate intimately in the mission whose origin is in the Father. *"Your first duty is to be with Christ. A constant danger for those who are engaged in apostolic work is to be so absorbed in the work for the Lord that they forget that the Lord is in the work."* For this reason, when you draw up the balance sheet of your apostolic tasks, always be sure to devote some moments of every day to personal and community prayer. These times of prayer must be carefully respected and be of appropriate duration; and, finally, do not hesitate to supplement them with periods of more intense meditation and prayer, setting aside specific times for that purpose. You must always make sure that the Eucharist is the natural center of your communities, and you will do this by fervent participation in daily Mass and by community prayer in chapels, where the Eucharistic presence of Christ expresses and fulfills what must be the principal mission of every religious family.

PHILIPPINES, FEBRUARY 17, 1981

The great evangelists have been principally interior souls, souls of prayer: they have always been able to find the time for prolonged meditation.

At the present moment, when you all have reason to suffer owing to the shortage of female apostolic workers, it is much better to pause and consider this truth, in the faith that "being" has greater value than "doing," which is always limited and imperfect. Be certain, furthermore, that your courageous and joyful fidelity to the fundamental requirements of the consecrated life will present an urgent invitation to young women, always ready to be generous, to follow the Lord on the path traced by you.

MAY 13, 1983

Prayer is an irreplaceable element of our vocation. It is so essential that for its sake other things—apparently more urgent—can and must be placed in the background. Even if your daily life in the service of mankind is overburdened with work, it has to include time devoted to silence and to prayer. Prayer and work must never be separated from each other. If we meditate every day and commend our work to God, it becomes prayer.

Learn to pray! For this, draw above all on the richness of the Liturgy of the Hours and the Eucharist, which should accompany your daily work in a special way. Learn to pray in the school of the Lord, so that you may become masters of prayer and able *to teach prayer* to those who are entrusted to you. If you teach men to pray, then you will restore the word to their faith, which is often shaken. Through prayer you will lead them back to God and return substance and meaning to their lives.

Austria, September 13, 1983

Meeting Christ in prayer

Religious consecration is in itself a way of participating profoundly in Christ's mission to save the world.

You will recall the priestly prayer of Jesus: *"Father... as thou hast sent me into the world, even so have I also sent them into the world. And for their sakes I sanctify myself, that they also might be sanctified through the truth."* This sanctification means spiritual offering and sacrifice, and total availability to the will of the Father, so that, through this complete giving, salvation may come to all men. Consecrated souls offer themselves to Christ in prayer and in the apostolate in order to advance the missionary work, whose purpose is adherence to the faith and conversion.

It gives me pleasure to note that the concern of your institutes is to work among the poor, in whom they recognize Christ. But to recognize Christ in the poor man, you must first of all meet him and know him in prayer: activity for the Lord must never let you forget the one who is the Lord of that activity, and who through the Holy Spirit brings forth his authentic fruit. The Code of Canon Law, the faithful interpreter of the Council's precepts, states it perfectly: *"The Apostolate of all the religious consists above all in the testimony of their consecrated lives which they are bound to preserve through prayer and repentance."*

And in the exhausting round of your apostolic tasks there must be, daily and weekly, attentive, prolonged periods of personal and community prayer.

MAY 22, 1986

I conclude by encouraging you to be men and women of *prayer,* because the Spirit of God must be the soul of your apostolate, permeate your thoughts, your desires, your actions, purify them, elevate them. Like priests and religious, lay people are called to holiness; prayer is the honored pathway. And then you have many occasions to thank and intercede for all those you are close to. I learn with great pleasure that there has been a true revival of prayer, which translates into, among other things, a flowering of prayer groups, but which also, I hope, informs the life of your movements. God be praised! May the Virgin Mary always accompany the apostolate that you perform in the name of her Son. And, in expressing my trust and joy, I bless you, along with all the members of your movements and your friends and families, from the bottom of my heart.

FRANCE, MAY 31, 1980

The Care of Vocations

There is an urgent need today for a more widespread and deeply felt conviction that all the members of the Church, without exception, have the grace and responsibility to look after vocations. The Second Vatican Council was quite explicit in declaring that *"the duty of fostering vocations belongs to the entire Christian community, which should discharge this task principally by living full Christian lives."* Only on the basis of this conviction will pastoral work on behalf of vocations be able to display its truly ecclesial aspect, develop a harmonious plan of action, and make use of specific agencies and suitable instruments of communion and co-responsibility.

PASTORES DABO VOBIS, 41

For everyone's benefit, let's recall the remarkable words of Paul VI, which can be adapted to every age in the life of the Church: "Do not forget, ever, the testimony of history: faithfulness to prayer or its abandonment is the test of the vitality or the decadence of the religious life" (*Evangelica testificatio,* 42).

SEPTEMBER 19, 1983

Craftsmen of evangelization

I would like to convey through you an exhortation to parents to support their children when they hear the Lord's call. I would like to ask that, by means of your vocation, you help others see the complete human fulfillment that is gained by the follower of Christ in the consecrated life. The Church, as you know, needs craftsmen dedicated to evangelization. Hence you must all be allies in promoting vocations, since the Lord continues to call those whom he wishes to share in his intimacy.

PERU, MAY 15, 1988

At the beginning I spoke to you of the marvelous gift we have received, of the divine call. I don't want to conclude this meeting without adding some words on the responsibility to promote new priestly vocations. This should be a concern of the first importance, manifested in our prayer and in our apostolate. I ask the Carmelite Virgin that your zeal and your example may inspire many souls to give themselves to Christ in the priesthood and the consecrated life. The Church needs them, in order to continue, in this new stage, the immense job of evangelization.

Holy Mary, intercede for us with your Son, and hear us!

CHILE, APRIL 1, 1987

Dear brothers: you have enriched the whole Church by responding to Christ's call to special service. You may be sure that the joy you feel and communicate to others, with the grace of Christ, will help promote vocations. It is not at all foolish to be "out of your mind for Christ." Communicate this message to others. Pray for vocations. Pray that parents may encourage their children to ask themselves if they have a vocation and to accept that challenge. The Lord Jesus needs you to carry out his plan for the salvation of the world.

Let us go forward, then, with faith in the love of God, with praise in our hearts.

AUSTRALIA, NOVEMBER 28, 1986

I am fully aware of your concern about the number of vocations to the religious life. It is undoubtedly a serious problem for many churches and local communities. In this regard Christ's words are a challenge to us; they demonstrate that prayer must be our first response to the shortage of vocations. We must ask the Holy Spirit to speak to the hearts of young people. And we must be sure that what we offer them is in fact the word and the challenge and the promise of Jesus.

Those whom Christ calls to your houses of formation have the right to receive the authentic teaching of the Church and a true understanding of the religious life. Only in this way will their consecrated love begin to belong fully to the Church and their apostolate be a fruitful vehicle of the grace of Christ for themselves and others.

The current problems are the Lord's method of calling on us to place greater faith in him, to be stronger witnesses to the wonder of his ways, and to have a deeper trust in him who alone is the master of our future. We have listened to the words of today's reading: *"God is faithful, by whom you were called into the fellowship of his Son, Jesus Christ our Lord."* God who is faithful will sustain you. He exhorts you to have trust in him.

AUSTRALIA, NOVEMBER 26, 1986

"Here I am, Lord! I am ready! Send me!"

Cooperation is expressed by promoting missionary vocations. While the validity of various kinds of missionary commitment should be recognized, at the same time *a full and lifelong commitment to the work of the missions should be given priority,* especially in the institutes and missionary congregations, male and female. Promoting such vocations is at the heart of cooperation: preaching the Gospel requires preachers; the harvest needs laborers. The mission is carried out, above all, by men and women who are consecrated for life to the work of the Gospel, and are prepared to go forth into the whole world to bring salvation.

I wish to call to your minds and recommend to you this *concern for missionary vocations.* We are aware of the overall responsibility of Christians to contribute to missionary work and to the development of poor peoples, and so we must ask ourselves how it is that in some countries, while monetary donations are increasing, missionary vocations, which are the true measure of self-giving to one's brothers and sisters, are in danger of disappearing. Vocations to the priesthood and the consecrated life are a sure sign of the vitality of a Church.

REDEMPTORIS MISSIO, 79

"The harvest is plentiful, but the laborers are few." The recruitment of *vocations* is close to our heart. On what pathways are we to find them? The Apostle Paul said: *"I therefore, a prisoner for the Lord, beg you to lead a life worthy of the calling to which you have been called."*

I wish to repeat that exhortation: the behavior that corresponds to your vocation—Christian, priestly, religious—is the origin of new vocations. This integrated behavior constitutes a permanent base for prayer: it prepares the ground, and prayer is its fruit; and, reciprocally, prayer consistently inspires this behavior.

Priests, deacons, and both male and female religious have a particular responsibility to inspire and sustain vocations. If they testify to the joy of serving Christ, if by their faith they radiate hope even in the midst of their labors, if they truly do their best for souls, if they can initiate them to prayer that pervades their very life, how, then, can we doubt that vocations will flower around them? We know young people, and many of them are looking for meaning in their lives. Let us invite them to contribute to our pastoral activities: liturgical celebrations, catechism, care of the poor and the sick, organization of movements. We invite them to share in our religious life: *"Come and see."* But we are also not afraid to call them explicitly to this service. Let us cease to be pessimistic, resigned, timid when we speak of vocations. Surely the seed exists in the hearts of many young people, and is only waiting for the opportunity to germinate.

And let's not forget this aim in our prayers: let us pray, and get others to pray, for priestly and religious vocations.

The entire Church truly needs such prayers. *"Pray therefore the Lord of the harvest to send out laborers into his harvest."*

Let us pray with Mary. She is the model of the life consecrated to the Lord. She directs the disciples toward Christ so that they may adhere to him, with love, and do all that he says. It is easy for us to say with her, in the "Our Father," *"Thy will be done."*

With Mary, we open our hearts to the *Holy Spirit.*

Let us pray in the name of Christ. Perhaps, up to now, invoking the name of Christ, you have not asked enough. Hold on to the conviction that *"with God nothing will be impossible."*

"Ask, and you will receive, that your joy may be full."

Yes, vocations are the fruit of prayer, they are the source of joy in the Church. Amen.

BELGIUM, MAY 18, 1985

Mary

The members of Secular Institutes, living their daily lives within the different strata of society, have in Mary an example and a help in offering the people with whom they share life in the world a sense of the harmony and beauty of a human existence that is the greater and more joyful the more open it is to God. They offer testimony of a life lived in order to build communities more and more worthy of the human being; and they offer proof that temporal realities, lived with the force of the Gospel, can give life to society, making it freer and more just, for the good of all the children of God, Lord of the universe and the Giver of every good thing. This will be the hymn that humanity, like Mary, raises to God, acknowledging his omnipotence and mercy.

If, with the expanded commitment undertaken in living your consecration fully, you consider the sublime model of she who was perfectly consecrated to God, the Mother of Jesus, and the Church, the effectiveness of your evangelical testimony will increase and, consequently, the *pastoral work on behalf of vocations* will benefit.

Many institutes, it's true, are today experiencing a serious shortage of vocations, and in many areas the Church warns of the need for a greater number of vocations to the consecrated life. So the Marian year could mark a revival of vocations through more trusting recourse to Mary, the mother who provides for the necessities of the family, and through an increased sense of responsibility on the part of all the ecclesial constituents for the promotion of the consecrated life in the Church.

JUNE 2, 1988

The Virgin continues to be the model for every consecrated person. She is the consecrated woman, the Virgin of Nazareth, who, listening, praying, and loving, was chosen to be the Mother of God. *"If the entire Church finds in Mary its primary model, you who are consecrated people and communities within the Church have even more reason to do so."*

Humble and forgetful of herself, Mary dedicated her life so that the will of the Lord might be fulfilled in her. Her life was placed in the service of God's plan for salvation.

She was truly happy and fortunate. Deprived of every power that did not come from the force of the Spirit that overshadowed her, she did not avoid the cross but lived in conjugal faithfulness to the Lord as a model and Mother of the Church.

May the Virgin accompany you always; may she teach you the path of faith and humble joy that comes of putting your existence in the service of the Kingdom; may she guide you and encourage you on the path of holiness and in your evangelical activities.

On this occasion I wish to address a special word of encouragement to the members of the Secular Institutes, who, with their style of consecrated life, affirmed by the Second Vatican Council, perform an extremely important service in the Church, responding to new apostolic challenges and being themselves the leaven of Christ in the world.

Your charism represents service of great value in today's world. Your apostolic activities glorify God and contribute effectively to the achievement of that civilization of love that is the divine plan for humanity, which awaits its glorious coming.

CHILE, APRIL 3, 1987

You must always be tenderly devoted to the Mother of God. Your piety toward her must preserve the simplicity of its first moments. May the Mother of Jesus, who is also our Mother, and who is the model of self-giving to the Lord and his mission, accompany you, make your cross gentle, and obtain for you, whatever your circumstances of life, that immutable joy and peace that only the Lord can give.

MADRID, NOVEMBER 2, 1982

I entrust you to her,
so that she may sustain and increase
your faithfulness to Christ
and the Church.
I ask her for
the abundant flowering and the ongoing
existence of vocations
for your religious families.
The Church needs your presence
to live this fulfillment of the Gospel.
May Mary,
the faithful Virgin,
solicitous of the needs of men,
concede to you this grace.
So let it be.

GUATEMALA, MARCH 7, 1983

I invite you to address Mary, Queen of the Apostles, so that she may enlighten, protect, and defend Christian families, from whom the vital sap of priestly and religious vocations flows.

The entire Church needs generous souls who are willing to spend all their energies for the Gospel. It's a serious problem that involves everyone, because it is on the presence of such souls, above all, that the Christian animation of society depends. It is a fundamental problem for the Church. The solution represents confirmation of her spiritual vitality and, at the same time, the state of that vitality; the state of her mission and its development.

During the joyous time of Easter, we contemplate Mary, the Queen of Heaven, beside her glorified Son; let us pray today and afterward for vocations in your communities and in the whole Church: may she inspire many, and obtain for them the light of the Holy Spirit.

VITERBO, MAY 27, 1984

In the Virgin of the Magnificat there are two remarkable kinds of faithfulness that are also a sign of your vocation: faithfulness to God, to his design of merciful love, and faithfulness to his people.

You, too, must be faithful to God and his design. Be faithful to your people. . . . Thus, like the Virgin of Nazareth, you will be God's collaborators, servants of your brothers and sisters, and better servants in a way *that is specifically yours:* bringing to all the message of Christ.

VENEZUELA, JANUARY 28, 1985

I commend you to the Virgin Mary, the Mother and the model for every consecrated soul. She inspires the abundant flowering of vocations to a life of special consecration, for the greater glory of God, the good of the Church, and service through love for mankind. May the Lord keep you always faithful to your vocation.

ECUADOR, JANUARY 30, 1985

In conclusion, dear brothers, I encourage you all to remain faithful to your charism, faithful to your vocation to holiness, faithful to your ministry of salvation: in this be inspired by Mary, the Mother of Christ. She encourages you through her example of faith; she sustains you through her faithful prayer. Your love, like hers, must be expressed in faith—faith in all that God asks of you through his Church: *Thy will be done!* For you faith is the condition by which you can contribute effectively to building the Kingdom of God; it is the premise for true sharing in the work of evangelization. The Incarnation of the Word was bound to Mary's faith, and the life of Jesus in the world is today bound to your faith. Without any doubt, your greatest contribution will be your love—a love that is manifested in lifelong faith in Jesus Christ and his Church.

NOVEMBER 26, 1981

O Mary,
Mother of Mercy,
watch over all people
so that Christ's cross was not in vain,
so that man does not stray from the path of the good,
or become blind to sin,
but so that he puts his hope ever more more fully in God
who is "rich in mercy."
May he carry out generously the good works
prepared by God beforehand,
and so live completely
"in praise of his glory."

VERITATIS SPLENDOR

Prayers

Dear brothers and sisters, it is with prayer that I would like to end these reflections suggested by the Gospel and your testimony.

Our Lord God, allow the visible and courageous presence of the consecrated in the world to be an eloquent sign of your love. Among the disciples you have chosen and established in the religious life, let the clarity of their message, the gift, without return, of themselves, the disinterestedness of their service, their faith in prayer be seen by young people as calls of your grace.

Let the institutes that have given so much to your Church see the flowering of numerous vocations, so their irreplaceable mission can continue.

Lord Jesus Christ, let those whom you have wished to call your friends know the fullness of joy that you have promised: the joy of praising you, the joy of serving their brothers and sisters, the joy of abiding in your love.

Let all your children who are members of the Secular Institutes, Lord, have the support of your grace and the abundance of your blessings.

FRANCE, OCTOBER 5, 1986

Lord Jesus, Good Shepherd, who offered your life so that all might have life, give us, a community of believers scattered throughout the world, the abundance of your life, and enable us to be witnesses of it and communicate it to others.

Lord Jesus, give the abundance of your life to all the people consecrated to you, in the service of the Church, make them happy in their giving, tireless in their ministry, generous in their sacrifice; and may their example open other hearts to hear your call and follow it.

Lord Jesus, give the abundance of your life to Christian families, so that they may be fervent in faith and in ecclesial service, thus encouraging the rise and development of new consecrated vocations.

Lord Jesus, give the abundance of your life to all the people, especially young men and women, whom you call to your service; enlighten them in their choices; help them in difficulties; sustain them in faith; make them ready and courageous in offering their lives, following your example, so that others may have life.

MESSAGE FOR THE WORLD DAY OF
PRAYER FOR VOCATIONS, 1982

Lord Jesus, hear our invocation:

- through your Spirit, renew your Church, so that it may with increasing fecundity offer to the world the fruits of your Redemption;
- through your Spirit, fortify in their holy purpose those who have dedicated their lives to your Church: in the Presbyterate, in the Deaconate, in the religious life, in the missionary institutes, in the other forms of consecrated life; you who have called them to serve you, make them full collaborators in your work of salvation;
- through your Spirit, multiply the calls to serve you: you read our hearts, and you know that many are disposed to follow you and work for you; give to young people and others, too, the generosity needed to welcome your call, the strength to accept the renunciations it requires, the joy of carrying the cross that is linked to their choice, as you carried it first, in the certainty of Resurrection.

We pray to you, Lord Jesus, together with your Most Holy Mother Mary, who was beside you in the hour of your Redeeming Sacrifice; we pray to you for her intercession, so that many among us, even today, may have the courage and the humility, the faith and the love to answer "Yes," as she did when she was called to collaborate with you in your mission of universal salvation. So let it be.

MESSAGE FOR THE WORLD DAY OF
PRAYER FOR VOCATIONS, 1983

Let us listen to the *words of our Lord Jesus Christ* who says: *"Lift up your eyes, and see how the fields are already white for harvest. He who reaps receives wages, and gathers fruit for eternal life, so that sower and reaper may rejoice together."*

And we ask—we ask him with all our soul for *this harvest,* just as he asked the Samaritan woman for living water, water for eternal life. And seeing that *"the fields are already white for harvest"* we know that there is a need for reapers, just as, earlier, there was a need for sowers. And we say to Christ that he has redeemed us with his Blood: Lord, here I am! Welcome me as sower and reaper of Your Kingdom, Lord, here I am! Send laborers for the harvest. *"Send out laborers into his harvest."*

MARCH 22, 1981

The Eucharist in the life of the consecrated

Keep alive the enthusiasm and joy of your consecration.
Grow in esteem and mutual help
Consider yourselves always and uniquely in generous service
*   to souls!*
And above all be profoundly Eucharistic souls!

*   John Paul II*

Lord, let us
find in the sacrifice of the Eucharist
the source of our pastoral charity.
Let our spirituality
be bound to the Eucharist.
From it let us obtain the strength
to offer our lives together with yours,
Highest Priest and victim of salvation.
Through the sacrifice of the Eucharist
the purpose of our virginity
is confirmed and reinforced,
so that nothing in the world
can make us stray from the path that leads to you.
Amen.

To Mary

The Christian is the man of the Annunciation.
With Mary, each of us and all together
desire to become "Men of the Annunciation."
                              John Paul II

O Mary,
your "YES" to God at the Annunciation
reminds us that we must respond
always more generously to the plans
that the Lord has for us.
Make our consecrated life
reflect your example:
that we, too, may open ourselves
to the action of the Holy Spirit
through our constant turning to Christ,
through our chastity, poverty, and obedience,
with the ceaseless rediscovery
of our vocation and mission in the Church.
Amen.

An offering of the self

O Lord,
may my soul
be flooded with your light
and know you more and more profoundly!
Lord,
give me so much love,
love forever, serene and generous,
that I will be united with you always!
Lord,
let me serve you
and serve you well,
on the pathways that you wish to open
to my existence here below.

I Would Like to Tell You Many Things....

I would like to tell you many other things, and I would like to hear from each of you your more personal concerns, but unfortunately I cannot prolong this meeting. I conclude by renewing my great faith in you, and with urging you to place faith in he who "*determines the number of the stars and gives to all of them their names,*" and who has called you by name, calling you from your mother's breast. Our love is radically placed in the "*preferential and consecrating love of God,*" who will not abandon those who turn to him with trust. For this reason, St. Paul reminds us that in all our tribulations "*we are more than conquerors through him who loved us.*" I end with this exhortation from the author of the Letter to the Hebrews: "*Therefore do not throw away your confidence, which has a great reward. For you have need of endurance, so that you may do the will of God and receive what is promised.*"

TERNI, MARCH 19, 1981

I wish to leave you a special command: follow Christ radically! Love for his person and devotion to his redemptive work constitute your choice in life. As far as the religious profession, you have chosen for him in a way so radical that *the inscrutable richness of Christ*" became the center and the measure of every other commitment.

Only in Christ and through him do you discern and carry out any choice, so that your service to your brothers and sisters passes for unconditional self-giving to Christ, your Lord and Bridegroom.

Radical dedication must guide you to an unreserved identification with Christ in his mystery of poverty, chastity, and obedience. This and none other must be the most intimate ecclesial focal point of the heart of the consecrated person and the source of his fecundity in the Church and in the world. The consecrated person's preferential love for Christ must animate and direct his whole life.

CHILE, APRIL 3, 1987

Christ needs you to build up His Kingdom

Allow me to go immediately to the heart of my message. Here it is: *Jesus Christ needs you to build his Kingdom on earth.* And the Church needs your special talents, as individuals and as communities, to carry out her mission of communicating Christ. In addition, millions of your colleagues, men and women, count on you to live an exemplary life, worthy of their human and Christian dignity.

PHILIPPINES, FEBRUARY 18, 1981

You are the future and the hope of the Church. The Church of the future will be better if you are better; the Church will be an evangelizing Church for the poor, if from this moment on you share your life with Christ, poor, obedient, and chaste; the Church of the year 2000 will be a missionary Church, if you will grow with a universal missionary spirit; a boundless spirit that is free and generous in self-giving to Christ who waits among your needy brothers and sisters. You will discover all this in "daily conversation" with Christ, your friend, who is present in the Eucharist and who follows you speaking, loving, and calling with the living and forever young word of the Gospel.

BOLIVIA, MAY 11, 1988

The era of missions is not over

The era of missions is not over;
Christ still needs
generous men and women
who will become messengers
of the Good News
to the ends of the earth.
Have no fear of following him.
Share freely with others
the faith that you have received!
"No believer in Christ,
no institution of the Church
can be separate from this supreme duty:
proclaiming Christ to all the people."

GAMBIA, FEBRUARY 23, 1992

Dear sons and daughters, your field of action, as you see, is vast. The Church expects much of you. It needs your testimony to bring to the world, famished for the word of God even if it doesn't know it, the "joyous message" that every authentically human aspiration can find its fulfillment in Christ. Know that you are at the height of the great possibilities that divine Providence offers you at the end of the second Christian millennium.

For my part, I renew my prayer to the Lord for the maternal intercession of the Virgin Mary, that she may grant you in abundance her gifts of light, wisdom, and determination as you search for better ways to be, among your brothers and sisters who are in the world, a living testimony rendered to Christ and a modest but convincing call to welcome his newness into personal life and social structures.

May the charity of the Lord guide your reflections. You will then be able to walk in faith.

AUGUST 28, 1980

Enroll yourself in the school of Christ

At the risk of being paradoxical, I ask that you permit the Pope, in all humility, for he knows your merits and your deep awareness, to invite you to enter the school of Christ. He is the "Teacher" for all of us. He is *the Way, the Truth, and the Light.* I pray to him for all of you, and for all those whom you represent, asking him to bless you, and assuring you again of my full trust.

APRIL 25, 1980

In my heart I have many other things that I would like to say to you, that I wish to communicate, except that I don't have time. I therefore renew my respect and my faith in all of you. To all I wish that *"your charity may be always richer in knowledge and in every sort of discernment; so that you may always be able to distinguish the best and be 'whole and irreproachable.'"*

BRAZIL, JULY 3, 1980

Appendix
Papal Documents

Christifidelis Laici (Lay Members of Christ's Faithful
People), Apostolic Exhortation, December 30, 1988
Catechesi Tradendae (On Catechesis in Our Time)
Apostolic Exhortation, October 16, 1979
Pastores Dabo Vobis (I Will Give You Shepherds),
Apostolic Exhortation, March 25, 1992
Redemptoris Missio (Mission of the Redeemer), Encyclical,
December 7, 1990
Mulieris Dignitatem (On the Vocation and Dignity of
Women), Apostolic Letter, August 15, 1988
Veritatis Splendor (The Splendor of Truth), Encyclical,
August 6, 1993
Evangelii Nuntiandi (On Evangelization in the Modern
World), Apostolic Exhortation of Paul VI, December 8,
1975

Special thanks to Rick Garson, chairman of Compulsion Entertainment. Thanks also to the Libreria Editrice Rogate (LER) and the Very Reverend Father Leonardo Sapienza, respectively, for the publication and the compilation of the anthologies. And to Alan R. Kershaw, Advocate of the Apostolic Tribunal of the Roman Rota, and Father Nunzio Spinelli for making this a global message.

KAROL WOJTYLA, POPE JOHN PAUL II, was born in Wadowice in Poland in 1920. He studied literature and drama in Krakow and later worked at a stone quarry and at a chemical plant. During the German occupation of Poland in World War II he began preparing for the priesthood and was ordained in 1946. Wojtyla became bishop of Krakow in 1958, archbishop in 1964, and cardinal in 1967. He was elected Pope in 1978 and is the 264th bishop of Rome.